DOUGLAS RODRIGUEZ'S LATIN FLAVORS ON THE GRILL

DOUGLAS RODRIGUEZ'S LATIN FLAVORS ON THE GRILL

with Andrew DiCataldo

Photography by Rodney Weidland

TEN SPEED PRESS

Berkeley   Toronto

This book is for the weekend warrior,
who, like me, loves to have an excuse to grill for a crowd of people.

—D. R.

~~~~~

Ten Speed Press
Box 7123
Berkeley, California 94707
www.tenspeed.com

Distributed in Australia by Simon & Schuster Australia, in Canada by Ten Speed Press Canada, in New Zealand by Southern Publishers Group, in South Africa by Real Books, in Southeast Asia by Berkeley Books, and in the United Kingdom and Europe by Airlift Book Company.

Cover and book design: Nancy Austin, Ten Speed Press
Author photograph on page 178 by Paulette Tavormina
Food and prop styling: Paulette Tavormina, Santa Fe, New Mexico
Introduction: Steve Siegelman, Berkeley, California

Special thanks to the following for prop loans and rentals: ABC Carpet & Home, New York, NY; Elizabeth Watt Studio, New York, NY; Hortensia Kreukels, New York, NY; and Paulette Tavormina, Santa Fe, NM.

Library of Congress Cataloging-in-Publication Data

Rodriguez, Douglas.

    Douglas Rodriguez's Latin flavors on the grill / with Andrew DiCataldo ; photography by Rodney Weidland.

    p. cm.

    ISBN 1-58008-055-3 (cloth)

    1. Barbecue cookery. 2. Cookery, Latin American. I. DiCataldo, Andrew, 1964- II. Title

TX840.B3 R625 2000

641.5'784--dc21   00-037792

Printed in Italy
First printing, 2000
1 2 3 4 5 6 7 8 9 10 — 05 04 03 02 01 00

ACKNOWLEDGMENTS

Thanks to all of my friends, neighbors, and the kids who contributed laughter and brightness to the many cookouts at my house throughout the summer of 1999, while I was working on this book. I especially want to thank my right-hand (wo)man, the indispensable Hortensia Kreukels, for all the hours she spent typing and reviewing the manuscript and page proofs, and for developing the dessert and bread recipes. (Hortensia was pastry chef to the late Felipe Rojas Lombardi, my mentor, and she teaches culinary arts at the New School in New York City in her spare time.)

My thanks also to all my sous chefs, Jason Bunin, Adrian Leon, Jorge Adriazola, Maximo Tejada, and Ramiro Jimenez; pastry chef Jose Luis Flores; and Donna-Marie Moore. Juventino Avila helped me make it through the photo shoot with his life-saving prep help. I am grateful to Lazaro Marron, Bruce Funk from the Long Island Beef Co., and Richard, and Robert, of Wild Edibles. I also wish to thank Stephan Bibeau and Roberto Dutesco of Skylight Six studio, and of course the amazing duo, photographer Rodney Wiedland and stylist Paulette Tavormina.

Most of all, thanks to my friends at Ten Speed: owner and world-class food lover Phil Wood, publisher Kirsty Melville, editorial director (and my editor) Lorena Jones, and art director (and my designer) Nancy Austin.

—Douglas Rodriguez

Writing this book involved hard work and the support and assistance of so many friends and family. I will be forever thankful to my wife, Patricia, for her encouragement, inspiration and understanding as I have pursued my goals throughout the years.

I would like to express my heartfelt thanks to my mother, Mary Ellen, and grandmother, Rose, for a lifetime of love and guidance.

I also owe special thanks to Hortensia Kreukels, for her outstanding contributions to the dessert chapter, and expert typing and refinement of the manuscript. She made all the difference in the world.

Thank you also to Jason Bunin for his contagious creativity and energy and to Lazaro Marron for his never-ending willingness to help with organizing and transporting ingredients for photo shoots.

Photographer Rodney Wiedland deserves an enormous thank you for his artistic ability to capture the beautiful images of food on film.

Thanks also to the entire crew at Ten Speed, especially Lorena Jones and Nancy Austin, for their exceptional editing and imaginative design, respectively, and to Phil Wood for always believing in Latin food.

And finally, I must declare my indebtedness to Douglas Rodriguez for his friendship and leadership, and for the opportunity to combine forces on this project.

—Andrew DiCataldo

CONTENTS

THE LATIN connection · THE GRiLL · THE TOOLS

THE FUEL · THE FUEGO · RUBS & MARiNADES

WORKING THE GRiLL · THE PARTY

introduction

As a first-generation Cuban-American, I grew up in a home filled with all the mouthwatering aromas, flavors, and passion of great Cuban cooking. But that home happened to be on Manhattan's Upper West Side, and there was no backyard, much less a backyard barbecue. My first real exposure to the heat of the grill didn't happen till I was a teenager and started working in restaurant kitchens. Ever since, it's always struck me as kind of funny that in the world of refinement and culinary artistry, there's basically this caveman act going on. Right in the middle of the finest professional kitchens, there's live fire. There's a glorified pit filled with glowing embers, and somebody's standing there poking raw meat with a fancy stick. Sure, the technique has gotten a little more refined over the last several thousand years. But even so, grilling is what it is.

To me, there's something really appealing about that. At my restaurants, I love to create exciting, surprising, inventive foods with colors and flavor combinations that blow people away. But at home, give me a sunny afternoon, a bunch of friends, and a bed of hot coals, and I'll give you a meal that's every bit as exciting and satisfying. And that's why I wrote this book. Basically, it was an excuse to have a huge party at my house every weekend and try out all these recipes. It's been a fun year.

Actually, ever since my wife, Trish, and I moved to Sleepy Hollow in Upstate New York, a few years ago, I've been making up for my lack of childhood barbecue experiences. As soon as the first thaw hits and spring starts sniffing around the corner, I'm out there with my wire brush and my spatula, ready for action. By the first of May, our freezer's stocked with ten racks of lamb, three dozen porterhouse steaks, and a pork loin or two—all marinated, portioned, and vacuum-packed. If we're in the mood for seafood, I'll grab some scallops, a little mahi mahi, or a couple of lobsters from the walk-in at the restaurant. By the time I'm home, Trish has the coals ready, and we can be sitting down to dinner in fifteen minutes. As long as the weather holds up, grilling is pretty much the only kind of cooking we do at our place. And the more I explore the joys of grilling, the more I'm convinced it's in my blood. It may have taken me a while to discover it, but there's something about cooking with fire that just feels instinctive.

THE LATIN CONNECTION

My family traveled a lot when I was growing up. We pretty much ate our way through the Spanish-speaking world, and I've been going back for seconds ever since. Which means I've had plenty of opportunities to check out Latin-style live-fire cooking.

In Ecuador, I've eaten succulent slices of pork roasted on spits over raging bonfires with flames leaping ten feet in the air. I've tasted meltingly tender flame-seared churrasco steaks glistening with emerald-green chimichurri sauce in Buenos Aires, and skewers of smoky grilled shrimp at a makeshift street stall in Peru.

Here's the thing: what makes this food so incredible is not so much the cooking method. In the end, fire is fire, whether you're in Toledo or Tierra del Fuego. The magic's in the rubs, marinades, and adobos, the sauces, mojitos, and salsas that can transform a nice steak or a fresh piece of fish into a Latin all-star.

That's good news for us North American backyard barbecuers. If you master the basic grilling techniques and combine them with the recipes in this book, you and your friends are in for some tasty Nuevo Latino eating.

marks, simply leave the food in one place until the marks appear, then rotate it 45° to create cross-hatched grill marks. Flip the food over to finish cooking, and then serve it marked-side-up.

Most chefs use their sense of touch to determine when foods are cooked and ready to come off the grill. With a little practice, so can you. Otherwise, avoid cutting into meat to see if it's cooked—you'll lose a lot of juices. The most reliable way to judge doneness is to use an instant-read thermometer, which you should insert lengthwise into the end of the meat. Some recommended temperatures: poultry, 180°F; beef (medium-rare), 155-160°F; pork, 160-170°F. Bear in mind that the temperature of grilled foods will go up about five degrees after you take them off the grill.

When a piece of meat or poultry comes off the grill, cover it loosely with foil and let it sit for five minutes before you carve it. This will allow the meat to re-absorb its juices and it will be noticeably more moist and tasty than if you slice it immediately.

THE PARTY

Grilling is my idea of the perfect way to entertain. Everyone gets to hang out in the fresh air, people eat in stages as the food comes off the grill, and that means all the stress of formal courses and "dinner party" etiquette are nowhere to be found. Plus, the cleanup's a lot easier, and if you play your cards right, you can actually be a part of the party instead of sweating away behind the scenes. All this requires is a little planning.

Most of the recipes in this book serve six to eight because this is food to enjoy with friends, and once you've got the grill going, it's no extra trouble to make a little extra. Worst case scenario, you've got some fantastic leftovers. For six to eight guests plus a few kids and maybe an unexpected last-minute brother-in-law, I'd figure three appetizers, two main dishes (I usually start with 8 to 10 ounces of raw meat per person), and two or three side dishes. A grill party is mix-and-match kind of eating—trust your instincts and put together a menu of things you love to eat.

Do as much as you possibly can the night before the party. Marinate the meats. Make the sauces and sides. Get the dessert going.

About 45 minutes before the guests show up, get the coals started and set out a bucket filled with iced beers and soft drinks. Have a pitcher or two of my refreshing coolers standing by in the fridge (most are nonalcoholic and make perfect openers for a midafternoon party). Put on some tunes and your best pair of sneakers and get ready to rhumba.

The "apps," if they're grilled, can go on right when people arrive. The sides can be made ahead and parked on the side of the grill (as their name implies). And your two main dishes can, in most cases, be grilled side-by-side at the same time. If you don't have room for everything, just cook some of each in stages and let people keep filling their plates.

The secret to enjoying yourself at a time like this is what chefs call "mise en place," or, as we say in the real world, having your act together. Bring everything you'll need out to a side table by the grill, so you don't have to keep running in and out of the kitchen every two minutes. This means your ingredients and garnishes, your tools, serving utensils, platters (have clean ones ready for serving, not the ones you used to bring the raw meat outside on), a cutting board, and a carving knife. Now all you have to do is stand there grilling, smiling, and soaking up the compliments.

Latin food is bold, fresh, intense, and lively. Grilling is too. Put them together and you've got an instant party. And if you ask me, that's just how life ought to be. I hope you and your crowd will have as much fun cooking and eating from this book as I've had putting it together. I can't wait to get started on the sequel.

DOUGLAS RODRiGUEZ'S

LATiN FLAVORS

ON THE GRiLL

DRINKS &
APPETIZERS

Culantro Limeade (page 6)

DRINKS

CRANBERRY-GUAVA COOLER ~ 6

RED MIST ~ 6

PASSION FRUIT CITRONADE ~ 6

CULANTRO LIMEADE ~ 7

COCONUT WATER COOLER ~ 7

GREEN APPLE–JALAPEÑO COOLER ~ 8

PINEAPPLE-MINT COOLER ~ 8

KIWI COOLER ~ 9

TAMARIND-VANILLA COOLER ~ 9

WATERMELON-STRAWBERRY COOLER ~ 11

CAPPUCCINO-STYLE EGG CREAM ~ 11

BACARDI COCKTAIL ~ 12

BUENA VISTA COCKTAIL ~ 12

FROZEN KIWI DAIQUIRI ~ 15

CAIPIRINHA ~ 15

APPETIZERS

ROASTED EGGPLANT, TOMATO,
AND GOAT CHEESE QUESADILLA ~ 16

QUESO FUNDIDO ~ 17

LOBSTER, CARAMELIZED ONION,
AND BRIE QUESADILLA ~ 17

FIRE-ROASTED CLAM-ONION
QUESADILLA ~ 19

SARDINES with Roasted Red Pepper,
Olive, and Caper Salsa ~ 33

FROGS' LEGS with Mango Barbecue Sauce ~ 34

SPICY, TANGY CHICKEN WINGS ~ 35

LOLLIPOP WINGS ~ 36

MARINATED CHICKEN LIVER SKEWERS
with Fig Marmalade ~ 38

CLAMS with Chipotle-Cachucha Mojo
and Bacon ~ 20

MUSSELS IN BANANA LEAVES
with Saffron-Lemon Butter ~ 23

ROASTED OYSTERS with Black Trumpet
Mushroom Mojo ~ 24

ALASKAN KING CRAB LEGS
with Farina Farfoa de Yuca ~ 24

CRAB AND CORN CAKES
with Lobster–Red Pepper Vinaigrette ~ 26

SUGARCANE-SKEWERED SHRIMP
with Lemongrass Mojo ~ 27

OCTOPUS SKEWERS
with Black Olive Sauce ~ 28

CALAMARI RELLENOS ~ 30

HONEY-, LIME-, AND RUM-GLAZED
SHRIMP ~ 31

FOIE GRAS with Dried Cherry and
Shallot Mojo ~ 39

SUGARCANE-SKEWERED PORK TENDERLOIN
STRIPS with Costa Rican Coffee Glaze ~ 41

BONELESS BEEF SHORT RIBS
with Opal Basil Chimichurri ~ 42

ANTICUCHOS ~ 45

CRANBERRY-GUAVA COOLER

Serves 8

Ocean Spray doesn't know what they've been missing. Forget cranapple. Cranguava is the best combination I've had. To scale the recipe up or down, simply increase or decrease the quantities of juices in equal proportions.

1 46-ounce bottle cranberry juice

4 12-ounce cans guava nectar

Ice, to serve

1. Mix the juices together and serve over ice.

RED MIST

Serves 1

With its blazing red color and bitter fruity flavor, Campari is the ultimate summer liqueur. When mixed with sparkling wine and sweet Cointreau, it assumes almost aphrodisiac properties.

4 ounces chilled cava (Spanish sparkling wine)
   or champagne

$^1/_2$ ounce Campari

1 ounce Cointreau

Splash of cranberry juice

Ice, to serve

Dried cranberries, to serve

1. Mix together the sparkling wine, Campari, and Cointreau in a pitcher. Add the splash of cranberry juice.

2. Pour over ice, garnish with dried cranberries, and serve.

PASSION FRUIT CITRONADE

Serves 12

When I first started working as a professional chef, I was frustrated by the lack of availability of tropical fruits and other ingredients common in Latin America. Passion fruit were one of those ingredients that I couldn't cook without, so I made it my mission to get them (and many other fruits and vegetables!) on the USDA-approved list of imported foodstuffs. Eight years later, passion fruit are found just about everywhere in fresh and even frozen pulp form. This drink always takes me right back to the hammock on the Costa Rican beach where I first enjoyed something like it.

15 fresh passion fruit

1 gallon water

1 cup superfine sugar

Juice of 5 oranges

Juice of 3 lemons

Ice, to serve

1. Cut the passion fruit in half, spoon out the pulp, and reserve.

2. In a saucepan, mix the pulp with 3 cups of the water and the sugar and bring to a boil. Lower the heat and simmer for 5 minutes. Turn off the heat, mix well, and strain out the seeds.

3. Combine the strained juice with the orange and lemon juice and mix well.

4. Serve over ice.

About Measurements for Drinks

The recipes in this chapter use measurements in ounces. The standard liquor jigger is $1^1/_2$ ounces (equivalent to 3 tablespoons), but they're also available in 1- and 2-ounce sizes.

CULANTRO LIMEADE

Serves 6

Raymond Mohan, who was my chef de cuisine at Aquarela, in San Juan, and is now in charge of sauces at my new restaurant, Chicama, was always trying to find new ways to quench our thirst in the searing tropical heat of Puerto Rico. One of his most delicious concoctions was this electric green limeade. Drink it as soon as it is made, because it will lose its intense color as it sits.

2 cups firmly packed culantro leaves
2 quarts ice water
1 cup superfine sugar
Juice of 5 ripe limes (about 1 cup)
Dash Angostura bitters (optional)
Ice, to serve

1. In a blender at high speed, purée the culantro leaves with 1 1/2 cups of the ice water and the sugar for about 2 minutes. Pour twice through a fine mesh strainer to remove any fibrous residue.

2. Mix in the remaining 6 1/2 cups of ice water, the lime juice, and Angostura.

3. Immediately serve over ice.

COCONUT WATER COOLER

Serves 1

This reminds me of Puerto Rico, where you see many of the street vendors chopping coconut meat (cocitos frios). At the restaurant, we buy young coconuts by the case and so, naturally, we make our own coconut milk by blending the water inside the coconuts and the meat. But the staff is always eager to drink the water, so sometimes Luis Lopez, one of the guys in the kitchen, makes this refreshing cooler for them. Young, or green, coconut still has the husk on the outside, which some believe works as a "filtering agent" for people with kidney problems. Because the flavor of the lime is best extracted through mashing in a mortar, this cooler has to be made one at a time. It's a great job for a guest who wants to help!

1 lime, cut into wedges
3 tablespoons superfine sugar
1 young (green) fresh coconut
Ice, to serve

1. In a mortar, thoroughly mash the lime with sugar.

2. Fill a glass with ice.

3. Crack the coconut open, pour the coconut water into the mortar, stir, and strain into the glass.

GREEN APPLE–JALAPEÑO COOLER

Serves 12

One of my favorite tricks is to use spices, herbs, and other flavorings, like chiles, in unexpected ways. The flavor of this drink is pure apple, but the aftertaste has a pleasing little kick from the jalapeño. Be sure to use Granny Smith apples, which have a distinctively clean, tart taste and give this drink its bracing green apple flavor.

6 pounds Granny Smith apples, cored removed
   (do not peel)
3 large jalapeño peppers, stemmed and seeded
Juice of 3 limes
2 quarts water
1 cup superfine sugar
Ice, to serve

1. In a juice extractor, juice the apples and jalapeños. Strain into a container, let rest, and remove any foam that rises to the top.

2. Transfer the juice to a pitcher. Add the lime juice, water, and sugar and stir well.

3. Serve over ice.

PINEAPPLE-MINT COOLER

Serves 12

Of all the coolers, this is my favorite! Andrew and I serve a lot of coolers at our cookouts because we do not allow our children to drink sodas and we think coolers are a healthy, fun substitute for them. On occasion, however, we do adulterate the cooler with vodka and rum. The first time we did that is when this one became my favorite.

3 ripe pineapples, peeled and diced
2 quarts water
1 cup superfine sugar
6 sprigs mint
Juice of 3 limes
Ice, to serve

1. In a juice extractor, juice the pineapples and reserve.

2. In a large pitcher, combine the water, sugar, mint, and lime juice. Add the pineapple juice.

3. Serve over ice.

KIWI COOLER

Serves 8

I was never crazy about kiwis until I had kiwi juice for breakfast each morning on a trip to Hawaii. The juice quickly became something to look forward to, and I have included this drink in my repertoire ever since. Surprisingly, the slightly sweet and sour flavor of the kiwi juice is evened out by the tart apple juice.

25 kiwis, skin removed
5 green apples, cored (do not peel)
Ice, to serve
1 quart seltzer water

1. Chill glasses.

2. In a juice extractor, juice the kiwis and apples.

3. Mix the kiwi and apple juice well.

4. Fill chilled glasses with ice. Pour in the juice to fill the glasses halfway, then top with seltzer.

TAMARIND-VANILLA COOLER

Serves 12

My introduction to tamarind goes back to my first chef job at the Wet Paint Café in Miami's South Beach district. The block behind the restaurant was lined with tamarind trees, and I never knew it until Bobbi, one of the prep cooks, brought in a bag full and made a "fabutastic" (as I like to say) drink with them that I have never forgotten. The addition of seductively aromatic vanilla is my touch.

1 (6-ounce) package tamarind pulp with seeds
1^1/$_2$ cups superfine sugar
1 gallon water
3 vanilla beans, pulp scraped out
Ice, to serve

1. In a saucepan, combine the tamarind pulp, sugar, and water. Bring to a boil and stir well to break up tamarind. Lower the heat and simmer for 5 minutes. Remove from the heat and stir well.

2. Strain into a pitcher and let cool.

3. When cool, stir in the vanilla pulp.

4. Serve over ice.

ERS

WATERMELON-STRAWBERRY COOLER

Serves 12

When we were kids, my brother, Frank, and I went to Miami Beach for summer vacation every year. One year our hotel room was on a high floor, and we remember sitting on the balcony slurping away on watermelon hunks and spitting seeds over the railing to rain down on the people walking along the street. Now that we have our own children, Frank and I make this cooler to give them a seedless version to enjoy—and hope that they won't resort to our antics!

5 pounds watermelon

5 pints strawberries, washed and hulled

Ice, to serve

2 quarts seltzer water

Tiny watermelon wedges and/or lemon wedges, to garnish

1. Cut the watermelon into pieces. Cut the rind off, slice the flesh into long, thin pieces, and remove the seeds.

2. In a juice extractor, juice the melon and strawberries and pour through a strainer.

3. Fill each glass three-quarters full with the juice, add the ice cubes and seltzer water, and stir.

4. Garnish with watermelon and/or lemon wedges and serve.

CAPPUCCINO-STYLE EGG CREAM

Serves 12

Egg cream originated here in New York, but I couldn't resist Latinizing it with two classic South American flavors: chocolate and coffee. When I have the time, I also like to jazz up the presentation by coating the rims of the glasses with a mixture of cocoa powder, sugar, and a little finely ground coffee. It's the best way I know to enjoy coffee on a hot summer day.

4 cups strong coffee, brewed and refrigerated until cold

2 tablespoons vanilla extract

$^1/_2$ cup superfine sugar

$^1/_2$ cup chocolate syrup

1 pint heavy cream, ice cold

1 quart seltzer water, ice cold

1. Combine the coffee, vanilla, sugar, and chocolate syrup in a pitcher. Mix well with a spoon until all the sugar is dissolved. Add the cream and seltzer.

2. Serve immediately in chilled glasses.

BACARDI COCKTAIL

Serves 1

This is a 1950s classic cocktail that my dad enjoys making and serving (even though he doesn't drink them himself!).

2 ounces Bacardi Limon
1 ounce lime juice
1 teaspoon Simple Syrup (see page 176)
1 dash grenadine
Ice
Lime slice, to garnish

1. Combine the rum, lime juice, simple syrup, grenadine, and ice in a cocktail shaker. Shake well and strain into a chilled martini glass.

2. Garnish with the slice of lime and serve.

BUENA VISTA COCKTAIL

Serves 1

With the rise of Latin restaurants everywhere and the country's new love affair with all things Cuban, everyone has reinvented this classic Cuban drink. But no one has recreated it the way my cousin John Hernandez did. I loved his version instantly because it's like a mojito-martini-margarita—three of my favorite drinks!

Juice of 1 lime
1 tablespoon superfine sugar
6 mint leaves
3 ounces Bacardi Limon
2 ounces club soda
1 scoop ice
Lime juice and sugar, to serve (optional)
Lime slice, to garnish

1. Combine the lime juice, superfine sugar, mint, rum, club soda, and ice in a blender and blend at high speed for 1 minute.

2. Rim martini glass with lime juice and sugar. Pour in cocktail and garnish with lime slice.

FROZEN KIWI DAIQUIRI

Serves 6

We developed this daiquiri to mark the end of another long day of recipe testing. The drink is based on the Kiwi Cooler (page 9), to which we added rum until it took on a life of its own. The full flavor of the kiwi dominates the rum, so it's easy to overindulge on these potent drinks.

25 kiwis, skin removed
10 ounces Bacardi Limon
4 tablespoons superfine sugar
Juice of 3 limes
4 ounces Midori
Ice cubes
1 lime wedge
Green decorator's sugar, to garnish (optional)

1. With a juice extractor or in a blender or the bowl of a food processor, juice the kiwis. (You should have 2 cups juice.)

2. Combine the kiwi juice, rum, sugar, lime juice, and Midori in a blender. Add ice to fill and blend well.

3. Rim glasses with juice from lime wedge and sugar.

4. Pour into chilled glasses and serve.

CAIPIRINHA

Serves 2

This refreshing drink is best served when the guest list is short because it's difficult to get the intense tangerine flavor out of the skins when mixing more than two at a time.

1 tangerine
2 tablespoons sugar
1 tablespoon lime juice
Ice, to serve
8 ounces Cachaça

1. Dice the tangerine with the skin on. Put half into a tall glass (bar glass) and add the sugar.

2. With a muddler or teaspoon mix the tangerine and sugar together so that the tangerine skins release their oil and the sugar dissolves.

3. Add the ice and Cachaça and divide into two glasses.

ROASTED EGGPLANT, TOMATO, AND GOAT CHEESE QUESADILLA

Serves 6 to 8

The combination of eggplant, tomatoes, and cheese in the filling makes this a tasty vegetarian quesadilla. The filling is delicious in empanadas, too. If you do not like goat cheese, substitute another soft cheese, such as farmer's or ricotta. Enjoy these quesadillas while still warm, along with a simple green salad.

ROASTED EGGPLANT FILLING

1 medium-size eggplant, sliced $1/2$ inch thick

2 tablespoons light olive oil

1 tablespoon ancho chile powder

1 teaspoon cayenne pepper

1 tablespoon garlic powder

2 teaspoons salt

$1^1/2$ teaspoons freshly ground black pepper

3 tablespoons canola oil

1 onion, cut into $1/4$-inch dice

3 tomatoes, cut into $1/4$-inch dice

2 tablespoons tomato paste

2 ounces soft goat cheese, crumbled

$1/4$ cup chopped fresh parsley

6 (10-inch) flour tortillas

$1/4$ cup Red Chile Oil (page 150)

1. Preheat the oven to 350°F.

2. To make the filling, brush the eggplant with the olive oil. In a small bowl, mix together the ancho powder, cayenne, garlic powder, salt, and pepper. Sprinkle the spice mixture over the eggplant slices, coating them evenly.

3. Heat a large skillet over high heat. Add the canola oil and heat until hot but not smoking. Add the eggplant slices. Pan roast, turning the eggplant with a spatula until the slices are dark brown on both sides. Transfer the eggplant to a shallow baking dish. To the same skillet, add the onion and sauté for 5 minutes. Add the tomatoes and tomato paste, stir, and cook for 3 more minutes.

4. Spoon the tomato-onion mixture over the eggplant slices and roast for 30 minutes. Remove from the heat and let cool.

5. When cool, transfer the eggplant slices to a cutting board and coarsely chop. Combine the chopped eggplant-tomato mixture in a bowl with the goat cheese and toss with parsley.

6. Prepare a medium-low fire in the grill.

7. To assemble the quesadillas, divide the eggplant filling into six portions, spreading them over one-half of the tortilla. Fold the tortillas over to form half circles. Brush the top and bottom of each tortilla lightly with the chile oil.

8. Carefully place the quesadillas on the hot grate and grill for 2 to 3 minutes. Flip with a spatula and grill for another 2 to 3 minutes, or until the tortillas are toasted and the fillings are hot.

9. Transfer the quesadillas to a cutting board and cut into quarters.

QUESO FUNDIDO

Serves 4

This is one of the easiest appetizers you can make for a grill party. You just pile all the ingredients in an earthenware dish and set it over the hot coals while you prepare something else. In this version, I use cheeses you are likely to have on hand, but anything goes. Really. And you can add in different types of sausage, chiles, vegetables—whatever you like. I like to scoop up this spicy, gooey cheese dip with tortilla chips or raw veggies.

2 roasted poblano chiles (page 179), peeled, seeded, and finely diced
6 sprigs cilantro, finely chopped
$1/2$ cup finely diced chorizo
$1/2$ cup finely diced plum tomatoes
1 cup shredded white Cheddar cheese
1 cup shredded Monterey Jack cheese
$1/2$ cup grated mozzarella cheese
3 tablespoons grated Parmesan cheese
Tortilla chips or cut-up raw vegetables, for serving

1. Prepare a medium fire in the grill, piling all the coals to one side or heating only one side of a gas grill.

2. In a large bowl, toss together the chiles, cilantro, chorizo, tomatoes, and cheese. Mix well and pour into an earthenware dish.

3. Place the dish on the grate over the side of the grill opposite the heat source for indirect heat. Cover the grill and roast for 5 minutes. When the cheese begins to bubble (which may take up to 8 more minutes), remove the dish from the grill.

4. Serve immediately with the chips or vegetables.

LOBSTER, CARAMELIZED ONION, AND BRIE QUESADILLA

Serves 6 to 8

This flavor combination first appeared as a pizza topping at the Wet Paint Café in Miami, where I had my debut as a chef, in 1986. It just goes to show that a flavor combination will stand the test of time when it's really good.

2 sweet (Vidalia, Maui, or Walla Walla) onions, sliced
2 tablespoons butter
2 tablespoons vegetable oil
6 (10-inch) flour tortillas
1 pound Brie cheese, sliced $1/4$ inch thick
1 pound cooked lobster meat, chopped
$1/4$ cup olive oil
Smoky Corn Salsa (page 170) or your favorite tomato-based salsa, to serve

1. In a sauté pan over medium heat, combine the onions with the butter and oil and sauté until the onions are dark golden brown and caramelized. Remove from the heat and allow to cool.

2. Prepare a medium-low fire in the grill.

3. To assemble quesadillas, divide the onions among the tortillas, spreading them over one half of the tortilla. Next, lay the Brie over onions, followed by the cooked lobster meat, and fold over to form half circles. Brush the top and bottom of each tortilla lightly with olive oil.

4. Carefully place the quesadillas on the grill and grill for 2 to 3 minutes. Flip with a spatula and cook for another 2 to 3 minutes, or until the tortillas are toasted and the cheese is melted.

5. Transfer the quesadillas to a cutting board and cut into wedges. Serve with the salsa.

FIRE-ROASTED CLAM-ONION QUESADILLA

Serves 6 to 8

Don't turn the page because this recipe looks involved. If you grill the onions and make the vinaigrette in advance (like the night before you entertain), the rest of the preparation comes together quickly. Be sure to buy and grill a few extra clams—they are completely irresistible hot off the grill, and you are bound to lose a few to hungry spectators.

CLAM-ONION FILLING

3 tablespoons thyme leaves, picked from stem

¹/₄ cup coarsely chopped flat-leaf parsley

¹/₄ cup coarsely chopped cilantro

3 cloves garlic, finely chopped

1 tablespoon crushed red pepper flakes

¹/₄ cup freshly squeezed lemon juice

¹/₂ cup olive oil

Sea salt

Freshly ground black pepper

48 littleneck clams, scrubbed

2 Spanish onions, sliced into ¹/₄-inch rings

1 pint very small cherry, grape, or teardrop tomatoes

¹/₂ cup finely diced celery

6 (10-inch) flour tortillas

1 pound shredded queso blanco or Muenster cheese

¹/₄ cup olive oil

Sour cream, to serve

1. Prepare a medium-hot fire in the grill.

2. Make a vinaigrette by combining the herbs, garlic, red pepper flakes, lemon juice, oil, and salt and pepper.

3. When the coals are ready, place the clams on a baking sheet, set on the hot grate, cover with the lid, and grill for 3 minutes. Remove the lid and discard any unopened clams. Recover and grill for 2 more minutes. Remove the clam meat from the shells, reserving it with all of the clam juice. Discard the shells.

4. Toss the onion slices in a small amount of the vinaigrette. Place them on the hot grate and grill until soft and browned, 7 to 8 minutes per side. Transfer to a cutting board, then dice and add to the clam meat with the remaining vinaigrette, cherry tomatoes, and celery. Season to taste.

5. To assemble quesadillas, divide the clam mixture among the tortillas, spreading it over one half of each tortilla. Sprinkle the cheese evenly over filling. Fold the tortillas over to form half circles. Lightly brush the top and bottom of each tortilla with olive oil.

6. Allow the fire to burn down to medium-low heat. Carefully place the quesadillas on the hot grate for 2 to 3 minutes. Flip with a spatula and grill for another 2 to 3 minutes, or until the tortillas are toasted and the cheese begins to melt.

7. Transfer to a cutting board and cut into wedges. Serve at once with a dollop of sour cream.

CLAMS WITH CHIPOTLE-CACHUCHA MOJO AND BACON

Serves 6 to 8

Here is a Latin-style version of clams casino that utilizes one of our favorite chiles, the cachucha, or ajicito. It is a mild chile pepper from the Dominican Republic, very fragrant with citrus overtones. Imagine the flavor of a habanero without the heat. Clams, such as littlenecks or cherrystones, are recommended for this recipe—anything bigger will become too tough. If you like the mojo here, try it with poultry, steak, pork chops, and any grilled fish.

CHIPOTLE-CACHUCHA MOJO

2^1/$_2$ chipotle chiles, toasted and minced

^{1}/$_4$ cup stemmed, seeded, and finely chopped cachucha peppers

2 tablespoons diced red bell pepper

2 tablespoons chopped scallions, white and green parts

2 tablespoons minced red onion

2 tablespoons minced garlic

2 tablespoons chopped cilantro

^{1}/$_4$ cup freshly squeezed lime juice

6 tablespoons light olive oil

Salt and freshly ground black pepper

8 ounces bacon, finely diced

4 dozen clams, scrubbed

1. To make the mojo, mix all the ingredients together in a bowl and set aside in the refrigerator.

2. Prepare a medium-hot fire in the grill.

3. Place the bacon in a saucepan and cook until crisp on the grill or on the stove. With a slotted spoon, transfer the bacon to a plate lined with a paper towel. Discard the bacon fat.

4. Arrange the clams on the hot grate and grill for 6 to 8 minutes, or until the shells open.

5. Transfer the clams to a serving plate and discard any clams that did not open. Spoon a teaspoon of mojo into the shells and sprinkle with crisp bacon. Serve immediately.

CLAMS WITH MOJO & BACON

Mussels in Banana Leaves
with Saffron-Lemon Butter

Serves 4

Banana leaves impart a slightly sweet and fruity green banana flavor to the foods cooked inside them. Fresh banana leaves offer a more concentrated flavor, but frozen banana leaves, sold in Asian, Mexican, and Latino markets, also work well.

SAFFRON-LEMON BUTTER

1 teaspoon saffron threads

1 cup dry white wine

3 cloves garlic, chopped

3 shallots, chopped

2 bay leaves

10 black peppercorns

1 pound unsalted butter, softened

Zest of 3 lemons

2 teaspoons freshly squeezed lemon juice

1 (16-ounce) package banana leaves

3 pounds mussels, scrubbed and debearded

6 sprigs thyme

1. To make the saffron butter, combine the saffron, wine, garlic, shallots, bay leaves, and peppercorns in a nonreactive saucepan. Over medium heat, reduce the volume to 1/4 cup. Discard the peppercorns and bay leaves.

2. Place the softened butter in a food processor. Add the saffron reduction, lemon zest, and lemon juice. Purée until the butter is smooth and takes on a bright yellow color. Place the saffron butter in a plastic container or roll up in parchment paper and set aside.

3. Prepare a medium fire in the grill with the coals all piled on one side of the grill or by lighting only one side of a gas grill.

4. Using scissors, cut each banana leaf to form a rectangle measuring 6 inches by 12 inches. Lay out the leaves and divide the mussels among them. Place a tablespoon of saffron butter in the center of each leaf with 1 or 2 sprigs of thyme. Fold up the sides and ends of each leaf to form a neat package. Wrap each package in aluminum foil.

5. Place the packages on the hot grate on the side of the grill opposite the heat source. Cover the grill and roast for 15 to 20 minutes, until the mussel shells open.

6. Transfer the packages to a plate, slit open the packages, and serve.

ROASTED OYSTERS
WITH BLACK TRUMPET MUSHROOM MOJO

Serves 4

The mojo reminds me of a mignonette. That is probably what put the notion in my head to pair it with oysters— raw and roasted. Enjoy the oysters with a dry white wine or, better yet, live it up with a glass of champagne.

2 dozen oysters in the shell, scrubbed
1/2 cup Shallot-Truffle Mojo (page 172)

1. Prepare a medium-high fire in the grill.

2. Arrange the oysters, rounded side down to retain juices, on the hot grate. Grill until the shells begin to pop open, 4 to 5 minutes.

3. Transfer the oysters to a serving platter and remove the top of the shells. Spoon a teaspoonful of mojo on each oyster and serve immediately.

ALASKAN KING CRAB LEGS
WITH FARINA FARFOA DE YUCA

Serves 4 to 6

Farina farfoa de yuca is a staple in Brazil, where it is made from the finely ground meal of the manioc root (aka cassava or yuca). The meal is usually toasted in a skillet with oil or butter, then sprinkled over rice, beans, fish, meat—just about anything and everything. It is found in Latin markets that sell Brazilian specialty foods. Mix about 3/4 cup breadcrumbs with 1/4 cup cornmeal, then toast to make a suitable substitute.

4 pounds Alaskan king crab legs
1/2 cup butter or olive oil
1 cup farina farfoa de yuca
1/4 cup finely chopped parsley
Salt and freshly ground black pepper
Lemon wedges

1. Using shears, cut along the outside of the crab legs on both sides, removing the top portion of the shell and leaving the meat resting on the lower half shell intact. Arrange the legs on a sheet pan and hold in the refrigerator.

2. Heat 1/4 cup of the butter or oil in a skillet over medium-low heat. Add the farina and toast, stirring constantly, for 4 to 5 minutes, or until well colored. Add the parsley and seasonings. Allow the seasoned crumbs to cool for a few minutes.

3. Prepare a medium fire in the grill.

4. Sprinkle the crumbs over the crab meat, then drizzle with the remaining 1/4 cup of melted butter or oil. Arrange the legs on the hot grate and heat through, 3 to 4 minutes.

5. Transfer to a serving plate and garnish with lemon wedges.

OYSTERS

CRAB AND CORN CAKES
WITH LOBSTER–RED PEPPER VINAIGRETTE

Serves 4

Everyone has a secret recipe for crab cakes. Well, my secret is the simple yet truly delicious vinaigrette I serve them with. It'll turn any fish or shellfish preparation into something special. Add some red chiles to spice it up, if you like.

LOBSTER–RED PEPPER VINAIGRETTE

1/4 cup lobster stock reduction
  (1 cup lobster stock, page 176, reduced to 1/4 cup)

1 large roasted red bell pepper (page 179)

2 tablespoons aged sherry wine vinegar

1 egg yolk

1 tablespoon olive oil

3 tablespoons canola oil

1/2 teaspoon salt

CRAB AND CORN CAKES

3 tablespoons olive oil

1/3 cup finely diced white onion

1/4 cup finely diced red bell pepper

1 teaspoon minced garlic

1/2 cup corn kernels

Salt and freshly ground black pepper

1/2 cup finely chopped scallions, white and green parts

2 eggs

1 tablespoon chopped chipotle peppers in adobo sauce

1 tablespoon Dijon mustard

1/2 cup dried unseasoned breadcrumbs

1 pound lump crabmeat, picked clean of shells

1 cup cornmeal

1/2 cup unsalted butter, melted

1. To make the vinaigrette, combine the stock, roasted pepper, and vinegar in a blender. Purée until smooth. Add the egg yolk and mix well. With the motor running, add the olive and canola oils in a slow steady stream until completely emulsified. Season with salt and set aside.

2. To prepare the crab and corn cakes, heat the olive oil in a large skillet over high heat. Add the onion, bell pepper, garlic, corn, and salt and pepper and sauté for 2 minutes. Add the scallions and cook 30 seconds longer. Remove the skillet from the heat and place the vegetables in a bowl to cool to room temperature.

3. Prepare a medium fire in the grill.

4. Combine the cooled vegetables with the eggs, chipotle, mustard, and breadcrumbs and stir well. Gently fold in the crabmeat. Using your hands, form the mixture into 8 to 10 crab cakes and dredge them in the cornmeal.

5. Lay a sheet of aluminum foil over the grate of your grill and brush with melted butter. Grill the cakes for about 3 minutes on each side, until light brown.

6. To serve, spoon some of the vinaigrette onto each plate and top with a crab cake.

SUGARCANE-SKEWERED SHRIMP with Lemongrass Mojo

Serves 6 to 8

One of my signature creations was tuna skewered with sugarcane. Borrowing on that concept, I use sugarcane instead of the usual bamboo skewers for my kabobs. The faintly sweet, rustic-looking spears add flavor and flair to my grill menus. Sugarcane is most commonly found in Latin and Asian markets. It can be stored in the refrigerator for approximately 1 month. Kaffir lime leaves may be substituted for the fresh lime leaves, which are also available in Latino markets. This mojo is also delicious over steamed or grilled shrimp and chicken, and adds a kick to pork tenderloin or chops. For a vegetable plate, it's an impressive final touch.

3 stalks lemongrass, trimmed

10 fresh lime leaves

1-inch piece fresh ginger

2 tablespoons rice vinegar

2 tablespoons sake

2 shallots

2 tablespoons fresh basil leaves, loosely packed

2 tablespoons fresh cilantro leaves, loosely packed

1/4 cup finely chopped chives

1 serrano chile

10 tablespoons honey

1/4 cup freshly squeezed lemon juice

1/4 cup vegetable oil

Salt and freshly ground black pepper

1 (12-inch) stick sugarcane

24 jumbo shrimp peeled and deveined, with tail shell intact

Salt and freshly ground black pepper

1. To make the mojo, thinly slice 2 lemongrass stalks, 6 lime leaves, and half of the ginger. Combine in a saucepan with the rice wine vinegar and sake. Over medium-high heat, cook until reduced by half, 12 to 15 minutes. Remove from the heat and leave to steep for 1 hour. Strain, reserving the liquid and discarding the solids.

2. While the lemongrass mixture steeps, finely mince the remaining 1 stalk lemongrass, 4 lime leaves, 1/2-inch piece ginger, and shallots, basil, cilantro, chives, and serrano chile.

3. Add the minced ingredients to the strained reduction. Stir in the honey, lemon juice, and vegetable oil. Season with salt and freshly ground pepper and mix well. Set aside.

4. Position the sugarcane stick standing upright vertically on a cutting board. With a sharp chef's knife, carefully cut the sugarcane in half lengthwise from top to bottom. Cut the pieces of sugarcane in half again lengthwise. Now you have 4 quarters. Cut each quarter in half again lengthwise to achieve 8 long, thin pieces of cane. With the tip of your knife, fashion a point on one end of each sugarcane skewer. Then, just above the shell of the tail, insert the skewer through the tail and continue through the thick, meaty part of the shrimp below the natural curve of the shrimp to secure it to the sugarcane. Thread 2 more shrimp on the same skewer and repeat with the remaining skewers and shrimp.

5. Prepare a medium-high fire in the grill.

6. Brush the grate of the grill with oil to prevent sticking. Season the skewered shrimp and arrange on the grate. Grill for 2 to 3 minutes per side.

7. Transfer the cooked shrimp skewers to a serving plate and drizzle with the mojo.

OCTOPUS SKEWERS
WITH BLACK OLIVE SAUCE

Serves 6 to 8

Octopus, or pulpo *as it is known in Spanish, easily assumes the flavors of the grill and the marinade it is paired with. This is my interpretation of a classic Peruvian favorite, octopus salad with black olive sauce.*

BLACK OLIVE SAUCE

$^1/_4$ cup olive oil

1 white onion, finely diced

1 tablespoon finely chopped garlic

2 tomatoes, peeled, seeded, and coarsely chopped

1 cup Niçoise or other black olives, pitted

6 anchovy fillets, chopped

4 peperoncini, minced

$^1/_4$ cup red wine vinegar

Freshly ground black pepper

OCTOPUS SKEWERS

2 pounds fresh octopus, cleaned and trimmed

1 gallon water

4 stalks celery, cut into $^1/_4$-inch dice

1 red onion, cut into $^1/_4$-inch dice

$^1/_2$ cup olive oil

Juice and zest of 1 lemon

$^1/_2$ cup coarsely chopped flat-leaf parsley

2 teaspoons salt

1 teaspoon freshly ground pepper

1 package bamboo skewers

1. To prepare the sauce, heat a medium-size saucepan over medium-high heat. Add the olive oil, onion, and garlic and sauté for 4 to 5 minutes, stirring, until the onion begins to brown. Add the tomatoes, olives, anchovies, peperoncini, and vinegar and continue to cook for another 10 minutes. Season with pepper. Pour into a blender, purée until smooth, and set aside.

2. In a medium stockpot over low heat, place the octopus, water, celery, and onion. Bring to a simmer cover, and cook for 1 hour. Remove from the heat and let the octopus cool in the water, about 2 hours. Soak the bamboo skewers in cold water. Prepare a medium-high fire in the grill.

3. Remove the octopus from the water and cut the tentacles away from the head (cutting as close as possible to the head). Spear the tentacles through the cut end with the skewers.

4. In a large bowl, combine the olive oil, lemon juice and zest, parsley, salt and pepper. Add the skewered tentacles and toss. Lightly oil the grate. Place the skewers on the grill and cook about 2 minutes per side, until octopus is evenly charred.

5. Serve immediately with the olive sauce on the side.

CALAMARI RELLENOS

Serves 6 to 8

If you're looking for an appetizer than can be prepared the night before you grill, this is one to consider. The stuffed squid need to firm up in the refrigerator for at least 6 hours before cooking so that they hold together well when placed on the hot grill grate.

2 pounds squid, cleaned

4 ounces smoked bacon, finely diced

4 shallots, finely chopped

2 cloves garlic, finely chopped

2 stalks celery, finely chopped

1 teaspoon crushed red pepper flakes

1 cup seasoned dried breadcrumbs

6 sprigs parsley, stemmed and finely chopped

6 sprigs thyme, picked and stemmed

Zest and juice of 2 lemons

1. Separate the tentacles from the body of the squid. Finely chop the tentacles and set aside.

2. In a medium-size sauté pan over medium heat, cook the bacon until crispy, about 6 minutes, tossing frequently. Add the shallots, garlic, celery, and crushed red pepper and continue to cook for 2 minutes. Add the breadcrumbs, tentacles, parsley, thyme, and lemon juice and zest. Mix well, remove from the heat, and let cool.

3. Open the cavity in the squid and stuff it with filling, but only up to $1/4$ inch from the top. Secure the opening with a toothpick, "sewing" it closed. Repeat this process until all of the filling is used up.

4. Refrigerate the squid for about 6 hours to firm up the filling.

5. Prepare a medium fire in the grill.

6. Lightly oil the cooking grate, arrange the squid on the grate, and grill for about 3 minutes per side. Remove from the grill with tongs and let cool slightly before slicing.

7. Serve immediately.

CALAMARI RELLENOS

HONEY-, LIME-, AND RUM-GLAZED SHRIMP

Serves 4

Honey, lime, rum and ginger all have uniquely pronounced flavors. But when combined in this glaze, the result is downright stunning. Grilled shrimp is not the only thing that benefits from this mouth-tingling glaze; enjoy it with scallops, lobster, tuna, and most any firm fish, plus chicken and pork.

HONEY, LIME, AND RUM GLAZE

1/2 cup freshly squeezed lime juice

1/2 cup dark rum

1 tablespoon freshly grated ginger

2 tablespoons cornstarch dissolved
  in 2 tablespoons lime juice

3/4 cup honey

Kosher salt and freshly ground black pepper

Zest of 2 limes

1/4 cup finely chopped cilantro

20 large shrimp, at least 16/20 size, peeled and deveined

2 tablespoons oil

Salt and freshly ground black pepper

1. To prepare the glaze, combine the lime juice, rum, and ginger in a medium-size saucepan. Bring to a boil over high heat. Whisk in the cornstarch mixture, honey, and salt and pepper to taste. Cook until thickened, 1 to 2 minutes. Remove from the heat and let cool completely, then stir in the zest and cilantro. Transfer to a container, cover, keep cool, and set aside.

2. Prepare a medium-hot fire in the grill.

3. Toss the shrimp with the oil, 6 tablespoons of the glaze, and salt and pepper to taste. Lay the shrimp on the hot grate and grill for 1 to 2 minutes on each side, brushing often with additional glaze, until the shrimp have turned bright pink on the outside and white on the inside.

4. Arrange the cooked shrimp on a platter and serve.

HONEY-, LIME-, AND RUM-GLAZED SHRIMP

SARDINES with ROASTED RED PEPPER, OLIVE, AND CAPER SALSA

Serves 6 to 8

The strong flavor of sardines is usually masked by flavors much stronger than the fish itself, like chiles and vinegar. I find that grilling them retains their characteristic flavor yet softens its intensity.

ROASTED RED PEPPER, OLIVE, AND CAPER SALSA

1 pint red pearl onions

1 tablespoon butter

¹/₄ cup extra virgin olive oil

4 large roasted red bell peppers (page 179), cut in ¹/₂-inch dice

¹/₄ cup finely diced black olives

¹/₄ cup pitted, julienned green olives

2 tablespoons sliced caperberries

2 tablespoons capers

1 tablespoon chopped garlic

2 tablespoons coarsely chopped cilantro

2 tablespoons coarsely chopped flat-leaf parsley

4 teaspoons aged sherry wine vinegar

Freshly ground black pepper

24 fresh sardines, cleaned, heads and tails left on

3 tablespoons olive oil

Salt and freshly ground black pepper

1. To make the salsa, cut away the stem end on the pearl onions with a small paring knife. In a bowl, cover the onions with hot water and let sit for 10 to 15 minutes to loosen skins. Peel.

2. Heat a skillet with the butter and 1 tablespoon oil over medium heat. Add the onions and sauté for 5 to 6 minutes, until the onions are lightly caramelized. Add the peppers, olives, caperberries, capers, garlic, cilantro, parsley, vinegar, and pepper. Set aside.

3. Rinse the sardines under cold water and dry with paper towels. Place in a nonreactive bowl and add the oil and seasonings. Toss to coat well.

4. Prepare a medium-hot fire in the grill.

5. Oil the grate. Arrange the sardines on the hot grate and grill for 4 minutes per side, until the skin is slightly charred and the flesh is white and no longer translucent.

6. Transfer the sardines to a serving platter, spoon the salsa over them, and serve at once.

FROGS' LEGS
WITH MANGO BARBECUE SAUCE

Serves 6 to 8

Frogs' legs are always a tough sell, which is too bad because they really are delicious and pick up the flavors of whatever they're cooked with. The barbecue sauce recipe makes more than you'll need for the frogs' legs because I always like to have a little extra on hand. It keeps in the refrigerator for up to 2 weeks and is perfect with grilled pork.

MANGO BARBECUE SAUCE

1 tablespoon Dijon mustard

4 cloves garlic, chopped

3 whole red jalapeño chiles, with seeds, diced

$^1/_2$ cup rice wine vinegar

1 teaspoon garlic powder

2 cups mango nectar

1 tablespoon light molasses

1 ripe mango, peeled and diced (1 cup total)

1 teaspoon crushed red pepper flakes

Juice of 2 limes

$^1/_4$ cup finely chopped cilantro

1 teaspoon finely chopped garlic

2 tablespoons oil

Salt and freshly ground black pepper

12 pairs frogs' legs

1. To make the sauce, combine all the ingredients in a medium-size saucepan over medium heat and bring to a slow boil. Lower the heat and let the mixture simmer for about 35 minutes. Remove from the heat and let cool completely. Purée in a blender. Set aside.

2. Prepare a medium fire in the grill.

3. In a bowl, combine the lime juice, cilantro, garlic, oil, and salt and pepper. Add the frogs' legs and marinate for about 10 minutes.

4. Oil the grate. Remove the legs from the marinade and arrange on the hot grate. Grill for 3 minutes, then brush on the barbecue sauce. Turn the legs with tongs and grill for 3 more minutes. Move the legs to a cooler part of the grill. Brush again with barbecue sauce and cover the grill. Roast the legs for another 5 minutes to cook through.

5. Liberally reapply sauce to the frogs' legs, transfer to a serving platter, and serve.

SPICY, TANGY CHICKEN WINGS

Serves 6

The best wings I've ever had were Sam DeMarco's, which he served at First Restaurant, New York. His wings inspired me to create my own. It is important that these wings marinate overnight so they can develop the full tangy and spicy flavor.

24 chicken wings (3 pounds), wing tips removed

MARINADE

$^1/_2$ cup distilled white vinegar

$^1/_2$ cup orange juice

Zest of 2 oranges

$^3/_4$ cup honey

8 cloves garlic

2 tablespoons coriander seeds, toasted

2 tablespoons cumin seeds, toasted

1 tablespoon dried oregano

1 tablespoon crushed red pepper flakes

$^1/_4$ cup cilantro leaves

2 tablespoons salt

$^1/_4$ cup thinly sliced scallions, white and green parts

1. Score the wings 3 times on each side.

2. In a blender, combine all the marinade ingredients and purée at high speed for 30 seconds. Reserve $^1/_4$ cup of the marinade, for basting the wings. Cover the reserved marinade and refrigerate. Place the wings in a bowl, pour the remaining marinade over, toss, cover, and refrigerate overnight.

3. Prepare a medium fire in the grill.

4. Drain the wings. Oil the grate. Place the wings on the hot grate and grill for 7 to 8 minutes per side, basting frequently with the marinade set aside for this purpose. To test for doneness, pry open one of the scores with a knife blade. There should be no blood on the bone and the wings should be brown and caramelized.

5. To serve, sprinkle with the scallions and arrange on a platter.

SPICY, TANGY CHICKEN WINGS

LOLLIPOP WINGS

Serves 6

Now this is my kind of lollipop! For these wings, I "french," or scrape away the meat from the narrow end of the bone to create a succulent bite of chicken at one end and a handle at the other. The wings need to be marinated overnight so that the meat develops the moist tenderness and delicate flavors that make them a hit every time.

24 chicken wing drumettes (winglet removed)

MARINADE
1 tablespoon saffron threads
1/2 cup freshly squeezed lemon juice
1 tablespoon grated lemon zest
2 cups buttermilk
1/2 cup finely chopped shallots
1 teaspoon aniseeds
3 cloves garlic
2 tablespoons salt

1. To prepare the chicken, make a small incision with a paring knife at the narrow end of the winglet. Scrape down on the bone, pushing the meat down to form a lollipop-like shape as the bone is exposed.

2. To prepare the marinade, soak the saffron threads in the lemon juice for 10 minutes. Combine with the zest, buttermilk, shallots, aniseeds, garlic, and salt in a blender and pulse for 30 seconds.

3. In a baking pan with sides, stand all the chicken wings straight up. Pour the marinade over the wings and refrigerate overnight.

4. Preheat the oven to 400°F. Bake the wings for 8 minutes only. Remove them from the oven and let stand for about 1 hour. This step is necessary to blanch the wings slightly and set their shape before they go on the hot grill.

5. Prepare a medium fire in the grill.

6. Drain the wings. Oil the grate. Place the wings on the hot grate and grill for about 10 minutes, turning them with tongs occasionally.

7. Transfer the wings to a serving platter and serve.

MARINATED CHICKEN LIVER SKEWERS WITH FIG MARMALADE

Serves 6

The marinade draws the musky flavor out of the liver, especially if you marinate it for the full 12 hours. Liver, like frogs' legs, is an acquired taste—some love it and others steer clear. But even the naysayers will like these decadent morsels, which, when paired with the fig marmalade, give liver a whole new flavor. These skewers turn out best when prepared over very intense heat.

MARINADE

$^1/_2$ cup soy sauce

$1^1/_2$ cups water

3 tablespoons light molasses

$^1/_2$ cup toasted walnut oil

2 tablespoons salt

1 teaspoon aniseeds

3 vanilla beans, scraped

1 tablespoon crushed red pepper flakes

1 teaspoon ground cardamom

1 teaspoon ground cinnamon

2 pounds chicken livers, washed and cut into quarters

FIG MARMALADE

3 tablespoons toasted walnut oil

1 cup diced red onion

4 shallots, julienned

3 cloves garlic

2-inch piece fresh ginger, grated

1 tablespoon cardamom seeds

1 pound dried Mission figs, chopped

1 cup dark rum

$^1/_2$ cup water

2 tablespoons honey

3 sprigs scallions, white and green parts
  very finely chopped

2 tablespoons chopped black olives

1. To make the marinade, combine all the ingredients in a blender and pulse about 4 times at high speed.

2. Presoak 20 skewers in water to cover. Skewer the chicken livers by placing about 6 pieces on each skewer. Put the skewers in a shallow pan. Cover with the marinade and refrigerate for at least 2 hours or up to 12 hours.

3. To make the marmalade, heat the walnut oil over high heat in a medium-size saucepan. Add the onion and shallots and cook for about 4 minutes, stirring. When they begin to become translucent, add the garlic. (The heat must remain sizzling hot to caramelize the onion mixture.) Cook for about 4 more minutes, then add the ginger, cardamom, and figs, stirring and cooking for 3 more minutes. Add the rum and water. Bring to a boil, reduce to a simmer, add the honey, and let cook for 15 minutes. Remove from the heat and let cool. When the fig mixture is cool, gently fold in the scallions and olives (so the color stays bright).

4. Prepare a medium fire in the grill. Oil the grate.

5. Place the skewers on the hot grate and grill for about 2 minutes per side.

6. Serve with the room temperature marmalade.

FOIE GRAS WITH DRIED CHERRY AND SHALLOT MOJO

Serves 4 to 6

Since the quality of foie gras is very important, I only use Hudson Valley Foie Gras, which, in my opinion, is the best available. I always use Grade A, which is reserved for the firmest foie gras. The mojo is wonderful with any foie gras, duck, pork, or chicken dish. It is also a delicious vinaigrette for greens. The mustard oil in the mojo is available from Indian markets and Dean & Deluca (see page 183). I've given the amounts for more cherry mojo than this recipe uses with the hopes that having extra in the refrigerator might make a spontaneous grill gathering possible. (It keeps for up to 2 weeks in the refrigerator.)

DRIED CHERRY AND SHALLOT MOJO

¹/₂ cup dried tart cherries

¹/₄ cup port wine

¹/₂ cup thinly sliced shallots

¹/₄ cup cherry syrup

¹/₄ cup red wine vinegar

2 tablespoons mustard oil

1 piece Grade A foie gras (about 1 pound), chilled

Salt and freshly ground black pepper

1. To make the mojo, soak the cherries in the port for 2 hours, until softened. Remove from the port with a slotted spoon and reserve the wine. With a large knife, roughly chop the cherries. Place the remaining port in a saucepan and reduce by half to a thick syrup. Add the port wine syrup to the cherries. Add the shallots, cherry syrup, vinegar, and oil. Mix well and refrigerate.

2. Prepare a medium-hot fire in the grill with all the coals piled on one side or by firing only one side of a gas grill.

3. Slice the foie gras, using a sharp knife dipped in ice-cold water between slices, in half and then into 1-inch-thick slices. (You want to be certain both the foie gras and the knife are cold.)

4. Sprinkle with salt and pepper. Oil the grate.

5. Place the foie gras on the hot grate opposite from the heat source for indirect heat and grill for 5 to 6 minutes per side. To test for doneness, insert a thermometer into the breast portion of the foie gras. It should read an internal temperature of 140°F.

6. To serve, place the foie gras on a plate, or on a piece of bread on a plate, and drizzle some cherry mojo over.

FOIE GRAS

SUGARCANE-SKEWERED PORK TENDERLOIN STRIPS WITH COSTA RICAN COFFEE GLAZE

Serves 6

With the popularity of mole, the Mexican sauce that takes days to make, I came up with this Costa Rican alternative. Follow the instructions perfectly because there is a fine line between the correctly reduced sauce and an overdone one, which has a bitter taste. Keep tasting the sauce as it cooks; the bitter flavor diminishes and the properties of an intensely flavored mole develop once the proper consistency has been achieved.

2 sticks sugarcane (each about 12 inches long)

2 (1-pound) pork tenderloins, silver skin removed, sliced into long strips $1/2$ inch thick

1 cup Costa Rican Coffee Glaze (page 157)

1. Prepare a medium fire in the grill.

2. To prepare the sugarcane, position a sugarcane stick standing upright vertically on a cutting board. With a sharp chef's knife, carefully cut the sugarcane in half lengthwise from top to bottom, and again in half lengthwise to make 4 quarters. Cut each quarter in half again to achieve 8 thin long pieces of cane. Repeat with the second stick to make a total of 16 skewers. With the tip of your knife, fashion a point on one end of each sugarcane skewer.

3. With one skewer in one hand and a tenderloin strip in the other, beginning at the tip of the loin, insert the point of the skewer through the meat, loosely threading the pork onto the cane in a ribbonlike fashion. Repeat with the remaining meat until all pieces are threaded onto the skewers.

4. Oil the grate. Place the skewers on the hot grate and grill for 2 minutes on one side, then brush with the glaze. Turn the skewers, grill for 2 more minutes, and brush well with the glaze.

5. Arrange on a platter and serve at once.

BONELESS BEEF SHORT RIBS
WITH OPAL BASIL CHIMICHURRI

Serves 4

These are the most tender, succulent, mouth-watering ribs you will ever have. I like to serve them with stacks of warmed flour tortillas, in which the meat can be rolled up to make quick sandwiches.

2 pounds boneless beef short ribs, trimmed and cut into 3-inch lengths

1 cup Barbecue Spice Rub (page 151)

1/4 cup canola oil

1 quart beef stock

1 cup red wine

3 celery stalks, chopped

2 carrots, chopped

2 onions, chopped

2 tablespoons minced fresh thyme

1 teaspoon salt

1 teaspoon freshly ground black pepper

OPAL BASIL CHIMICHURRI

1/4 cup red wine vinegar

2 cloves garlic

1 jalapeño

2 dried bay leaves, crumbled

Salt and freshly ground black pepper

1/4 cup chopped opal basil leaves

1/2 cup olive oil

1. Prepare a medium fire in the grill.

2. Place the ribs in a bowl and toss with the spices and oil, rubbing it in with your hands. Oil the grate. Arrange the seasoned ribs on the hot grate and brown evenly on all sides for about 10 minutes.

3. Transfer the ribs to a roasting pan and add the beef stock, wine, celery, carrots, onions, thyme, salt, and pepper. Bring to a boil on your grill or stovetop, lower the heat to a simmer, and braise the ribs until fork-tender, about 1 1/2 hours.

4. While the ribs are braising, prepare the chimichurri. Combine the vinegar, garlic, jalapeño, bay leaves, and salt and pepper in a blender and purée until smooth. Pour into a bowl and stir in the basil and olive oil. Set aside.

5. Using tongs, remove the ribs from the roasting pan and place on a serving dish. Strain the braising liquid and reduce to thicken. Adjust the seasoning and pour over the ribs. Drizzle the chimichurri over the ribs and serve immediately, passing the leftover chimichurri at the table.

ANTICUCHOS

Serves 6

Anticucho is the name of a specific Peruvian dish that consists of marinated, skewered, and grilled beef hearts. However, now in Peruvian cuisine, anticucho refers to any protein that is marinated, skewered, and grilled. Charbroiled beef heart on a skewer is the most common traditional appetizer in Peru. Before you immediately dismiss this recipe, take my word for it that like other inexpensive, underused ethnic meats, such as tripe, the flavor and texture of heart is uniquely satisfying. When grilled, the heart meat becomes tender and its earthy qualities are most evident. It almost tastes like beef. The trick to achieving this is twofold: the marinating time and cutting the meat into small pieces, which produces tender, succulent skewers. It's important to start the day before you plan to serve the skewers. You'll need to allow time for the chiles to refresh in the beer before making the marinade, and then also for the skewers to marinate overnight in the refrigerator.

MARINADE

4 aji panca, seeded and stemmed

3 cups chicha de jora (Peruvian corn beer) or substitute 1$^1/_2$ cups beer and 1$^1/_2$ cups apple cider combined

2 tablespoons toasted coriander seeds

1 tablespoon toasted cumin seeds

6 cloves garlic, peeled

6 sprigs thyme, leaves picked off

6 sprigs cilantro

2 tablespoons salt

1 beef heart, washed and cut into $^1/_2$-inch cubes

Huacatay Aji (page 161), to serve

1. To make the marinade, soak the aji panca in the beer for about 2 hours.

2. Combine the coriander and cumin seeds with the soaked aji pancha and beer in a blender. Add the garlic, thyme leaves, cilantro, and salt. Pulse 3 times at high speed. Reserve $^1/_4$ cup of the marinade, for basting. Cover and refrigerate. Set aside the remaining marinade.

3. Place 4 to 5 pieces of the heart on each of 10 presoaked skewers. Place in a shallow pan, pour the remaining marinade over the skewers, cover, and refrigerate overnight.

4. Prepare a hot fire in the grill.

5. Oil the grate. Place the skewers on the hot grate and grill for 3 minutes on each side.

6. Brush with the marinade reserved for basting and serve on a platter with the Huacatay Aji.

FISH & SEAFOOD

FİSH

MAHI MAHI
with Chipotle Mayonnaise ~ 54

MAHI MAHI
with Pomelo–Red Onion Salsa ~ 55

SALMON with Dill Chimichurri ~ 57

PANELA- AND RUM-CURED
SMOKED SALMON ~ 58

SALMON with
Calabaza–Pumpkin Seed Mojo ~ 59

SEAFOOD

ROSEMARY-SKEWERED GRILLED SEA SCALLOPS
with Pine Nut–Raisin Compote ~ 49

SEA SCALLOPS with
Saffron–Aji Amarillo Sauce ~ 51

SHRIMP with Avocado-Horseradish Salsa ~ 51

GRILLED LOBSTER
with Coconut-Ginger Mojo ~ 52

TUNA with Mango-Ginger-Lime Mojo ~ 60

TUNA with Tomatillo-Avocado Salsa ~ 62

CHILEAN SEA BASS
with Tangerine-Serrano Mojo ~ 63

ROSEMARY-SKEWERED GRILLED SEA SCALLOPS
WITH Pine Nut–Raisin Compote

Serves 4

These scallop skewers are as easy to make as they are wonderful to eat. The sweetness of the sherried raisins, offset by the tangy lemon, helps bring out the perfume of the rosemary. The pine nuts provide a nice textural contrast to the meaty scallops. Grilled Mushroom and Malanga Salad (page 105) goes well with this.

18 sea scallops

3 tablespoons freshly squeezed lemon juice

4 tablespoons olive oil

Salt and freshly ground black pepper

$^1/_2$ cup pine nuts

1 cup raisins

1 cup sweet sherry

6 large sprigs rosemary, 6 to 8 inches in length

1. Remove the small tough muscle from the side of each scallop. Rinse the scallops under cold running water and pat dry with paper towels. Place in a bowl, add the lemon juice, olive oil, and salt and pepper. Toss the scallops to coat and let marinate for 20 minutes.

2. Prepare a hot fire in the grill.

3. Place the pine nuts in a sauté pan and set it on the hot grate. Toast the pine nuts, continuously moving and shaking the pan to evenly toast them, until golden brown. Remove from the pan and set aside. In the same warm sauté pan, combine the raisins and sherry. Bring to a boil and continue to cook until the raisins are plump and the sherry is reduced to a thick, glossy, sticky compote, or when the sauce coats the back of a spoon. Stir in the toasted pine nuts and reserve until later.

4. Remove the scallops from the marinade and reserve the marinade. With a scallop in one hand and a rosemary sprig in the other hand, begin to thread the scallop sideways onto the rosemary. Arrange 3 scallops on each skewer.

5. Oil the grill grate. Arrange the skewers on the grate and grill for 1 to 2 minutes per side, brushing with the reserved marinade. The scallops are done when they are firm and no longer translucent.

6. Transfer to a serving dish, spoon the compote over the scallops, and serve.

GRILLED SEA SCALLOPS

SEA SCALLOPS with
Saffron–Aji Amarillo Sauce

Serves 4

Aji amarillo is a chile from Peru. It is available in powder and paste form in jars and supplies a sharp, fiery heat with fragrant citrus notes. To complete the Peruvian theme, serve with Peruvian Sarsa Salad (page 112).

20 fresh sea scallops
2 tablespoons finely chopped cilantro
2 tablespoons oil
Kosher salt and freshly ground black pepper
Saffron–Aji Amarillo Sauce (page 175)

1. Prepare a medium fire in the grill. Set a grilling basket on the grill grate.

2. Remove any tough muscle on the side of each scallop. Place the scallops in a bowl and toss with cilantro, oil, and salt and pepper.

3. With tongs, arrange the scallops on the hot grate and grill for 2 to 3 minutes on each side. Keep a watchful eye on them since a hot fire will cook them quickly, and you should remove them from the grill while they are still a little translucent inside.

4. To serve, spread some of the sauce on 4 plates and place 5 scallops on each. Serve immediately.

SHRIMP with
Avocado-Horseradish Salsa

Serves 6

The salsa was born one day when we wanted a spicy avocado condiment for a pan-seared tuna tortilla wrap. Wasabi came to mind initially, then we realized we didn't have any on hand. The obvious alternative was freshly grated horseradish. I am glad we used it instead, because it produced an appealingly pungent but mellow flavor. If you like it here, try it on a cold roast beef or chicken sandwich or with chilled shrimp cocktail.

AVOCADO-HORSERADISH SALSA
4 ripe, firm Hass avocados, cut in $1/2$-inch dice
1 red onion, finely diced
$1/4$ cup chopped chives
$1/4$ cup freshly grated horseradish
1 cucumber, peeled, seeded, and finely diced
Juice of 2 lemons
2 tablespoons distilled white vinegar
$1/4$ cup cilantro leaves
Salt and freshly ground pepper

36 large shrimp, at least 16/20 size, peeled and deveined
2 tablespoons oil
Salt and freshly ground black pepper

1. To prepare the salsa, combine all the ingredients in a bowl and mix well, but gently. Cover with plastic wrap and refrigerate.

2. Prepare a medium-hot fire in the grill.

3. In a bowl, toss the shrimp with the oil and salt and pepper. Arrange on the hot grate and grill for 1 to 2 minutes per side, until the shrimp have turned bright pink on the outside and white on the inside.

4. To serve, place a large dollop of the salsa in the center of each of 6 plates and set 6 shrimp with tails up around the salsa on each plate.

GRILLED LOBSTER
with Coconut-Ginger Mojo

Serves 4

The coconut milk in the mojo adds a sweetness that pleasantly intermingles with that of the lobster, while the ginger adds a clean, pure burst of flavor. Serve with chunks of steamed yuca and Grilled Hearts of Palm and Cherry Tomato Salad (page 120). The coconut-ginger mojo is also great drizzled over grilled shrimp, scallops, lobster, tuna, salmon, or your favorite fish.

COCONUT-GINGER MOJO

1 cup unsweetened shredded coconut

2 (14-ounce) cans coconut milk

2 tablespoons freshly grated ginger

1/4 cup freshly squeezed lime juice

4 roasted red jalapeño chiles (page 179), peeled, seeded, and finely diced

1/2 cup coarsely chopped cilantro

1/2 cup thinly sliced scallions, white and green parts

1 tablespoon sugar

2 tablespoons Lemon Oil (page 150)

1 tablespoon finely minced garlic

4 live Maine lobsters, 1¹/4 to 1¹/2 pounds each

1 cup butter, melted

Salt and freshly ground black pepper

1. To prepare the mojo, combine the coconut, coconut milk, ginger, lime juice, jalapeños, cilantro, scallions, and sugar in a bowl. Set aside. In a small sauté pan over medium heat, heat the oil. Add the garlic and sauté for 1 minute, stirring constantly. Scrape the garlic and oil into the coconut mixture and mix well. Set aside.

2. To prepare the lobsters, place one facing you on a cutting board. With the tip of a sharp heavy knife, split the body and head in half with one swift and forceful motion, where the tail meets the body. (The lobster will now be dead.) Turn the lobster around facing the opposite direction and, in the same manner, cut the tail in half lengthwise. Now, with the backside of your knife, tap the claws until their shells crack. With your fingers pull the gray papery head sac out, as well as the intestines that run along the top portion of the tail halves. Separate the claws from the body. The lobster is now ready for the grill. Repeat with the remaining lobsters.

3. Prepare a hot fire in the grill.

4. With a brush, liberally apply melted butter to the exposed meat of the tail and the cracked openings of the claws. Season with salt and pepper. Arrange the lobster pieces on the hot grate, cut sides down, and grill for 6 to 8 minutes. Turn over to the shell side and grill another 6 to 8 minutes, basting often with butter. The lobster is done when the raw, opaque flesh becomes firm and white.

5. Transfer the lobsters to individual plates and serve immediately with the mojo on the top or to the side.

GRILLED LOBSTER

Mahi Mahi
with Chipotle Mayonnaise

Serves 6

The customers and staff always love the chipotle mayonnaise. It is such a versatile condiment that I use it on sandwiches, hot dogs, and even brush it on corn on the cob. You'll probably find dozens of uses for it, too. For a slight flavor variation, add a squeeze of fresh lime juice.

CHIPOTLE MAYONNAISE

1/2 cup mayonnaise

2 tablespoons finely chopped chipotles in adobo sauce

Salt and freshly ground black pepper

6 (6-ounce) fillets mahi mahi

2 tablespoons oil

Salt and freshly ground black pepper

1. To make the mayonnaise, combine the mayonnaise and chipotles and mix thoroughly. Add salt and pepper to taste and set aside.

2. Prepare a medium fire in the grill. Set a grilling basket on the grill grate. Oil the rack.

3. Brush the fillets with oil and season with salt and pepper. Place the fish fillets on the hot rack and grill for 4 to 5 minutes, until the fish is lightly browned on the outside and firm and white on the inside. Using tongs or a spatula, carefully turn the fillets and continue to grill for another 3 to 4 minutes.

4. Transer to serving plates, brush the mayonnaise on the mahi mahi (or serve on the side), and serve at once.

MAHI MAHI WITH
POMELO–RED ONION SALSA

Serves 6

Adrian Casho, a tropical fruit and vegetable supplier, does his very best to keep me informed about exotic, interesting produce. One day he brought by some pomelos that were successfully harvested in the Dominican Republic. (They are native to Asia and Malaysia, and are also known as shaddock.) This fruit is similar to pink grapefruit, except it may have six more segments than regular grapefruits and it is much sweeter. Plus, the pulp can be segmented easily without losing much juice. The rind can be as thick as $1/2$ inch, which I make into candied pomelo peels.

POMELO–RED ONION SALSA

3 pomelos (or substitute pink grapefruits)

1 red onion, thinly sliced

2 tablespoons coarsely chopped flat-leaf parsley

$1/4$ cup coarsely chopped cilantro

2 tablespoons sliced Pickled Jalapeños (page 177) with juice

$1/4$ cup grapeseed oil

6 (6-ounce) mahi mahi fillets

2 tablespoons olive oil

Salt and freshly ground black pepper

1. To prepare the salsa, juice one of the pomelos and set aside. With a sharp knife, cut away the thick rind from the remaining 2 pomelos. With your hands, begin to separate the segments. Then remove the pith and any membranes and separate the pulp into small clusters. Mix the juice and pulp with the onion, parsley, cilantro, jalapeños, and oil. Cover with plastic wrap and refrigerate.

2. Prepare a medium-hot fire in the grill. Set a grilling basket on the grill grate. Oil the rack.

3. Brush the fillets with olive oil and season with salt and pepper. Place the fillets directly on the hot rack and grill for 4 to 5 minutes on one side. Turn the fish, cover the grill, and cook for an additional 3 to 4 minutes, until the fish is lightly browned on the outside and firm and white on the inside.

4. Transfer to serving plates, spoon the salsa over the mahi mahi, and serve at once.

MAHI MAHI WITH POMELO–RED ONION SALSA

PANELA- AND RUM-CURED SMOKED SALMON

Serves 6

Panela is raw sugarcane. It has a sweet molasses- or caramel-like flavor that marries well with the rum. If you cannot find panela, just substitute dark brown sugar and molasses. The curing step takes at least 24 hours, so plan to start this recipe the day before you grill. This cure is also suitable for smoking marlin, pork tenderloin, and duck breast.

Habanero Satanico Aji (page 166)

PANELA-RUM CURE

6 allspice berries

6 star anise

2 tablespoons coriander seeds

3 chipotle chiles, dried or in adobo

2 bay leaves

1/2 cup sugar

3/4 cup kosher salt

1/2 cup grated panela or 1/2 cup brown sugar combined with 2 tablespoons molasses

1 vanilla bean, split lengthwise

1 cup dark rum

1/2 cup brandy

6 (6-ounce) salmon fillets

1. To make the aji, heat the oil in a sauté pan over medium heat. Add the onions, garlic, and habaneros for about 3 minutes. Add the coriander and panca chiles, and sauté for 1 more minute. Remove from heat and let cool. When the mixture has cooled, add the remaining ingredients, transfer to a jar, and refrigerate until ready to serve.

2. To prepare the cure, combine the allspice, anise, coriander, and dried chipotles (do not add chipotles in adobo) in a skillet over medium heat. Toast until fragrant, about 2 minutes. In a saucepan, combine the toasted spices with the chipotles in adobo, if using, and the bay leaves, sugar, salt, panela, vanilla bean, rum, and brandy. Bring to a boil over high heat, stirring to dissolve salt and sugars and to cook out the alcohol, about 5 minutes. Remove from the heat and add 5 to 6 ice cubes to cool it down.

3. When the cure is completely cool, pour it over the salmon in a nonreactive baking dish, cover, and refrigerate for at least 24 hours.

4. The next day, remove the salmon from the cure and pat dry with paper towels.

5. Prepare a hot fire in the grill with the coals piled up on one side of the grill, or by firing only one side of a gas grill.

6. Toss a handful of presoaked wood chips onto the fire. Arrange the salmon on the grate opposite the heat source for indirect heat. Cover the grill and smoke the fish for 10 to 12 minutes, adding wood when necessary (if the smoke diminishes). The fish is done when the flesh flakes easily when pressed lightly with the spatula.

7. Transfer to serving plates, and serve, passing the aji at the table.

SALMON WITH
CALABAZA–PUMPKIN SEED MOJO

Serves 6

Calabaza, also known as West Indian pumpkin, is a common ingredient in Latin cuisine, mostly in soups and stews. However, as always, I try to come up with new, interesting ways to prepare staples. Over the years, I've served calabaza a thousand different ways, but I've always liked this recipe because the smooth, tender flesh contrasts with the crunch of the pumpkin seeds and the roasted pumpkin seed oil links them both together. Do not hesitate to use this mojo in other ways, such as with pumpkin soup or chicken.

CALABAZA–PUMPKIN SEED MOJO

$1/2$ cup calabaza (West Indian pumpkin), peeled, seeded, and diced very small

1 red onion, finely chopped

$1/4$ cup finely chopped chives

1 poblano chile, finely diced

$1/4$ cup cilantro leaves

1 tablespoon chopped fresh marjoram

$1/3$ cup pumpkin seeds (pepitas), lightly toasted and coarsely chopped

1 teaspoon minced garlic

$1/4$ cup roasted pumpkin seed oil

Juice of 2 limes

$1/2$ teaspoon ground cumin

$1/2$ teaspoon dried oregano

$1/2$ teaspoon ground ancho chile

Kosher salt and freshly ground black pepper

6 (6-ounce) salmon fillets, skin left on

2 tablespoons oil

Kosher salt and freshly ground black pepper

1. To make the mojo, bring a small pot with salted water to a boil. Add the calabaza and blanch for 3 to 4 minutes, until tender but firm. Immediately drain and plunge into ice water. Drain again. Combine the calabaza with the onion, chives, poblano, cilantro, marjoram, pumpkin seeds, garlic, pumpkin seed oil, lime juice, cumin, oregano, ground ancho, and salt and pepper. Mix well. Set aside.

2. Prepare a medium-high fire in the grill.

3. Brush the salmon fillets with oil and season with salt and pepper. Lightly oil the grate. Place the fish, skin side up, directly on the grate and grill for 3 to 4 minutes. Turn the salmon over to the skin side, cover the grill, and finish grilling for 3 to 4 more minutes. The fish is done when the flesh flakes easily when pressed lightly with the spatula.

4. Transfer to serving plates, spoon the pumpkin seed mojo over the salmon (or serve on the side), and serve at once.

TUNA with
Mango-Ginger-Lime Mojo

Serves 6

Bold, Asian-inspired flavors come together in this very refreshing mojo, which I use to liven up the grilled tuna, and also to transform any ordinary pork loin, chicken breast, or scallop into something exotic. I add the mojo to everything from cold soup to sorbet. Try it as a dressing for lobster salad or stone crab. It's the dried mango and crystallized ginger that heighten and intensify the flavors.

MANGO-GINGER-LIME MOJO

1 cup mango juice

1/2 teaspoon minced fresh ginger

2 ripe mangoes, peeled and cut into 1/8-inch dice

3 scallions, thinly sliced

1 red bell pepper, cut into 1/8-inch dice

2 tablespoons minced dried mango

1 teaspoon minced crystallized ginger

1/4 cup freshly squeezed lime juice

2 tablespoons minced cilantro

1 serrano chile, minced

1/4 cup canola oil

Pinch salt

3 tablespoons oil

Kosher salt and freshly ground black pepper

6 (6-ounce) tuna steaks, cut 1-inch thick

1. To make the mojo, combine the mango juice and fresh ginger in a saucepan and bring to a boil. Continue boiling to reduce by half, approximately 5 minutes. Remove from the heat and let cool completely.

2. Add the diced mango, scallions, bell pepper, dried mango, crystallized ginger, lime juice, cilantro, chile, canola oil, and salt. Set aside.

3. Prepare a medium fire in the grill.

4. Oil and season the tuna steaks, arrange on the hot grate, and grill for 2 to 3 minutes per side for rare, 4 to 5 minutes per side for medium rare, and 6 to 7 minutes per side for well done.

5. Transfer the fish to serving plates, spoon some mojo over each tuna steak, and serve immediately.

TUNA with

MANGO-GINGER-LIME MOJO

TUNA WITH
TOMATILLO-AVOCADO SALSA

Serves 6

Tomatillos are used raw in this recipe to provide a sweet and tart flavor and striking emerald-green brilliance to the salsa. Diced avocado neutralizes the heat of the chiles, while providing a textural contrast to the grilled tuna. Bacon-Wrapped Cauliflower with Red Chile Oil and Lemon (page 103) or Quinoa Shrimp Salad (page 116) make great side dishes for the tuna. The salsa is really versatile and you can serve it chilled with any grilled fish, chicken, or pork loin chops.

TOMATILLO-AVOCADO SALSA

16 tomatillos, husked and washed

1/4 cup freshly squeezed lemon juice

1 ripe, firm Hass avocado, cut into 1/4-inch dice

1 poblano chile, seeded and minced

1 jalapeño chile, seeded and minced

1 small white onion, finely diced

2 cloves garlic, minced

2 tablespoons chopped cilantro

1/4 cup Garlic Oil (page 151)

Salt and freshly ground black pepper

6 (6-ounce) tuna steaks, cut 1 inch thick

3 tablespoons oil

Kosher salt and freshly ground black pepper

1. To make the salsa, place 8 of the tomatillos in a blender with the lemon juice and 2 tablespoons water. Purée well and pour into a bowl. Dice the 8 remaining tomatillos into small dice. Add to the puréed tomatillos, along with the avocado, poblano, jalapeño, onion, garlic, cilantro, garlic oil, and salt and pepper to taste. Set aside.

2. Prepare a medium fire in the grill.

3. Oil and season the tuna steaks, arrange on the hot grate, and grill for 2 to 3 minutes per side for rare, 4 to 5 minutes per side for medium rare, and 6 to 7 minutes per side for well done.

4. Transfer to serving plates, spoon salsa over the tuna, and serve immediately.

TUNA WITH TOMATILLO-AVOCADO SALSA

CHILEAN SEA BASS
WITH TANGERINE-SERRANO MOJO

Serves 6

*Chilean sea bass is, without a doubt, one of my cus-
tomers' favorite fish. In this recipe, the delicate, buttery
richness of the fish is cut nicely by the citrus mojo. The
grill actually caramelizes the exterior of the fish, giving it
a crisp texture in contrast to the soft, flaky interior.*

TANGERINE-SERRANO MOJO

12 tangerines

2 serrano chiles, finely chopped

4 shallots, finely minced

3 tablespoons chives, finely chopped

1 roasted red bell pepper (page 179), peeled, seeded,
  and finely diced

1/4 cup freshly squeezed lime juice

1/4 cup Lemon Oil (page 150)

1 tablespoon chopped parsley

1 tablespoon chopped cilantro

6 (6-ounce) fillets Chilean sea bass

2 tablespoons oil

Kosher salt and freshly ground black pepper

PICTURED ON PAGES 46–47

1. To prepare the mojo, extract the juice from 10 of
   the tangerines, strain, and pour into a small
   saucepan. Gently reduce the liquid by half to concentrate the tangerine flavor. Place the reduced
   juice in a bowl to cool.

2. With a sharp paring knife, cut away the rind of the
   2 remaining tangerines to expose the pulp, then
   cut between the segments alongside the thin
   membrane to remove the segments. Discard any
   seeds and add the tangerine segments to the bowl
   of juice. Add the chiles, shallots, chives, roasted
   pepper, lime juice, lemon oil, parsley, and cilantro.
   Mix well and set aside.

3. Prepare a medium fire in the grill.

4. Brush the fish with oil and season with salt and
   pepper. Place the fish on a hot grate directly over
   medium heat and grill to a golden brown on one
   side, about 3 to 4 minutes. Carefully turn the fish
   with a spatula, cover the grill, and continue to grill
   for 3 to 4 minutes, until the fish is no longer
   translucent and begins to flake.

5. Transfer to serving plates, spoon the mojo over the
   sea bass, and serve at once.

CHILEAN SEA BASS WITH TANGERINE-SERRANO MOJO

MEAT &
POULTRY

POULTRY

ANGEL'S DEVILISH DRUMSTICKS ~ 67

CHICKEN BREAST with Huitlacoche Sauce
and Smoky Corn Salsa ~ 68

CHICKEN SALAD with Ginger Vinaigrette ~ 69

TURKEY TENDERLOIN with Mole Rub ~ 71

DUCK BREAST with Balsamic-Pear Mojo ~ 72

TURKEY STEAKS with Cranberry Mojo ~ 73

PAELLA CLASSICAL ~ 75

CORNISH GAME HENS
with Honey-Mustard-Garlic-Cilantro Glaze ~ 76

MEAT

CUBAN BURGERS ~ 78

BUTTERFLIED LEG OF LAMB
with Peruvian Chicha de Jora Marinade ~ 79

LAMB LOIN with
Plantain and Pine Nut Crust ~ 81

PORK CHOPS with
Okra, Corn, and Jalapeño Salsa ~ 82

QUICK PORK TENDERLOIN CHURRASCO
with Fava Bean, Pozole, and Poblano Salsa ~ 83

PORK TENDERLOIN
with Aji Amarillo–Pineapple Mojo ~ 84

BABY BACK RIBS in Rain Forest Glaze ~ 86

HAM STEAK with
Grilled Pineapple-Tomatillo Salsa ~ 87

STRIP STEAK with Horseradish-Parsley Mojo ~ 89

GRILLED PORTERHOUSE STEAK
with Venezuelan Guasaca Sauce ~ 90

NICARAGUAN-STYLE CHURRASCO ~ 92

BEEF TENDERLOIN
with Shiitake Mushroom Mojo ~ 93

SMOKED FRONTIER BUFFALO RIB EYE
with Grilled Plantains ~ 95

ANGEL'S DEVILISH DRUMSTICKS

Serves 4 to 6

These drumsticks are named for a food runner, who was one of my first employees when I moved to New York. He often had a few free minutes while he was waiting for the plates to come out of the kitchen, so he spent the time concocting various salsas and hot sauces, which we would use on chicken for staff and family meals. Here is an adapted version of one of his best.

MARINADE
4 cloves garlic

2 tablespoons fresh thyme leaves

1/4 cup freshly squeezed lime juice

2 tablespoons paprika

1/4 cup honey

3/4 cup red hot sauce, such as Tabasco

3 smoked chipotles in adobo sauce

Kosher salt and freshly ground black pepper

16 chicken drumsticks

1. Combine all the marinade ingredients in a blender and purée until smooth.

2. Place the drumsticks in a nonreactive container, pour the marinade over them, and marinate in the refrigerator for at least 8 hours or, even better, overnight.

3. Prepare a medium fire in the grill.

4. Remove the chicken from the marinade and pat dry with paper towels. Place the drumsticks on the hot grate, cover, and grill for 20 minutes, turning frequently, until they are fully cooked through.

5. Transfer to a plate and serve.

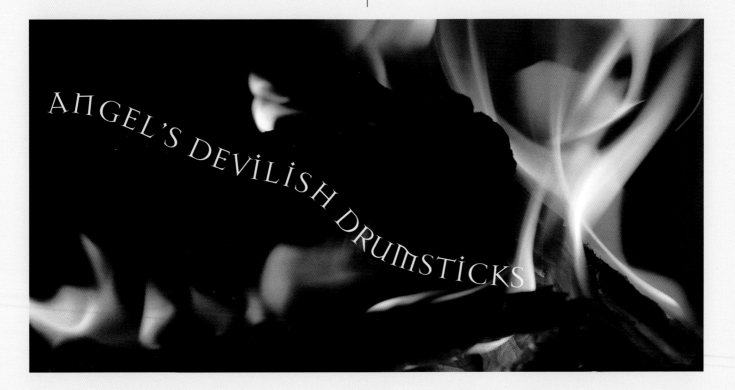

ANGEL'S DEVILISH DRUMSTICKS

CHICKEN BREAST
with Huitlacoche Sauce and Smoky Corn Salsa

Serves 6

Huitlacoche is a mushroomlike fungus that develops in the kernels of corn, morphing them into irregularly shaped gray-black mounds. It grows during the rainy season in Mexico and Guatemala. Huitlacoche may not look appealing, but its earthy, trufflelike flavor with sweet corn overtones makes a great mojo for cheese quesadillas or grilled chicken breast. You can also purée the sauce and add it to soup for an exotic flavoring. It is always aggressively seasoned with salt to neutralize its natural metallic taste. An herb called epazote is commonly used in most every preparation of the "black corn mushroom."

MARINADE
4 cloves garlic

1/2 white onion, coarsely chopped

1 teaspoon ground cumin

1 jalapeño chile, coarsely chopped

1/4 cup chopped cilantro

Juice of 1 lemon

Salt and freshly ground black pepper

1/2 cup vegetable oil

6 boneless, skinless chicken breasts

2 cups Smoky Corn Salsa (page 170)

1/2 cup crumbled queso blanco

HUITLACOCHE SAUCE
1/4 cup corn oil

1 onion, cut into 1/4-inch dice

3 garlic cloves, finely chopped

1 red bell pepper, cut into 1/4-inch dice

1 poblano chile, cut into 1/4-inch dice

1 jalapeño chile, with seeds, finely chopped

1 pound fresh huitlacoche

1 ripe tomato, cut into 1/4-inch dice

2 tablespoons chopped fresh epazote
  (substitute a mixture of cilantro and parsley)

1/4 cup vegetable or chicken stock (optional)

Kosher salt to taste

1. Combine all the marinade ingredients in a blender or food processor, and purée until smooth. Place the chicken breasts in a nonreactive container, pour the marinade over, and marinate in the refrigerator for at least 2 hours, but no more than 8 hours.

2. To make the sauce, place a medium-size saucepan over high heat. Add the corn oil, onion, and garlic. Cook for 2 minutes, stirring. Add the bell pepper, poblano, and jalapeño. Cook for 2 more minutes. Add the huitlacoche and cook for 2 more minutes. Lower the heat and add the tomato and epazote. If a thin sauce consistency is desired, add the stock. If a thick, stewlike consistency is desired, omit the stock. Continue to cook for 5 minutes. Season with salt. At this point, the sauce may be puréed or left chunky. Set aside.

3. Prepare a medium fire in the grill.

4. Remove the breasts from the marinade and pat dry with paper towels. Place the chicken on the hot grate and grill for 5 to 6 minutes on each side. The chicken should be thoroughly cooked, but still juicy, not dry.

5. To serve, spoon the corn salsa in the center of each of 6 plates. Slice the cooked chicken breasts and fan out over the salsa. Ladle the huitlacoche sauce around and sprinkle crumbled cheese over. Serve immediately.

CHICKEN SALAD
WITH GINGER VINAIGRETTE

Serves 6 to 8

This is a very healthy, low-fat, yet satisfying salad that I include in every barbecue party. Why? Because the wives tell us to!

4 boneless skinless chicken breasts

1 cup Ginger Vinaigrette (page 158)

1 cup sugar snap peas

1 pound blue potatoes

1 cup pearl onions, peeled

8 ounces asparagus spears

2 tablespoons oil

Salt and freshly ground black pepper

1 head frisée, cut into bite-size pieces

10 ounces spinach, stemmed

$^1/_2$ cup toasted pumpkin seeds (page 179)

1. Combine the chicken and $^1/_2$ cup of the vinaigrette in a nonreactive container and marinate in the refrigerator for at least 4 hours, but no more than 24 hours.

2. Blanch the sugar snap peas in a pot of boiling salted water for 2 minutes. Drain, plunge into ice water to stop the cooking, and drain again.

3. Boil the potatoes in salted water until tender, 15 to 20 minutes. Drain and allow to cool. When cool enough to handle, peel and slice $^1/_2$ inch thick.

4. Prepare a medium fire in the grill.

5. Remove the chicken from the marinade and pat dry with paper towels. Grill the breasts for 5 to 6 minutes on each side, until thoroughly cooked. Cut the chicken into $^1/_2$-inch cubes and set aside.

6. In a small bowl, toss the pearl onions and the asparagus with 2 tablespoons oil, salt, and pepper. Grill them over low heat, turning until the vegetables are lightly charred. Transfer the asparagus to a cutting board and cut into $1^1/_2$-inch pieces.

7. Combine the grilled vegetables with the diced chicken, frisée, spinach, sugar snap peas, potatoes, and remaining $^1/_2$ cup vinaigrette. Season with salt and pepper and toss well.

8. To serve, spoon the salad onto serving plates. Sprinkle with the toasted pumpkin seeds.

CHICKEN SALAD

WITH

GINGER VINAIGRETTE

TURKEY TENDERLOIN
WITH MOLE RUB

Serves 6

Plantains with Balsamic-Basil Glaze (page 107) are a great accompaniment and the Cranberry Mojo (page 73) is also delicious with the turkey. When I was in Dallas to do an event with our good friend, Dean Fearing, chef at the Mansion on Turtle Creek, Dean was kind enough to invite us to his Super Bowl party, where we ate, among many other good things, the most fantastic mole-rubbed pork tenderloin. As Dean would say, "Oh, Gawd that was gooood!" Here's a version Dean would be proud of.

6 turkey tenderloins
6 tablespoons vegetable oil
6 tablespoons Mole Rub (page 151)

1. Rub the tenderloins with the oil, then rub with the mole seasoning to completely cover. Refrigerate for 1 to 2 hours.

2. Prepare a medium-low fire in the grill.

3. Place the tenderloins on the hot grate for 10 to 12 minutes, turning frequently.

4. Transfer the cooked turkey to a cutting board and slice into 1/4-inch round slices.

5. Fan out the turkey slices on serving plates and drizzle with the mojo.

DUCK BREAST
WITH BALSAMIC-PEAR MOJO

Serves 6

Just before you serve this dish, take a moment to enjoy the wonderful aroma of the dried orange peel combined with the smokiness of the grill. The aroma is further enhanced by the fruity fragrance of the white grape vinegar, which gets its dark color and pungent sweetness from years of aging in barrels of various woods. This balsamic pear mojo is also incredible with squab and recipes that include blue cheese.

3/4 cup Orange-Coriander Adobo (page 152)
6 boneless, skinless duck breasts

BALSAMIC-PEAR MOJO
2 cups balsamic vinegar
1 white onion, cut into 1/8-inch dice
1/4 cup hazelnut oil
Salt and freshly ground black pepper
1 ripe pear, peeled, cored, and cut into 1/4-inch dice

1. Generously and liberally apply the adobo seasoning to both sides of each breast. Cover and refrigerate for at least 8 hours, or even better, overnight.

2. To make the mojo, combine the vinegar and onion in a small sauté pan. Bring to a boil and boil gently to reduce to 1/2 cup. Remove from the heat and let cool. In a slow steady stream, whisk in the oil, beating with a wire whisk in a slow steady motion. Season to taste with salt and pepper and fold in the diced pears. Set aside.

3. Prepare a medium fire in the grill.

4. Place the breasts on the hot grate and grill for 4 minutes. Turn over to cook an additional 4 minutes for medium-rare. The meat should be slightly pink and juicy.

5. Transfer the duck to a cutting board and allow the meat to rest for 2 minutes before slicing. With a sharp knife, cut thin slices against the grain. Transfer the slices to individual serving plates and spoon the mojo around.

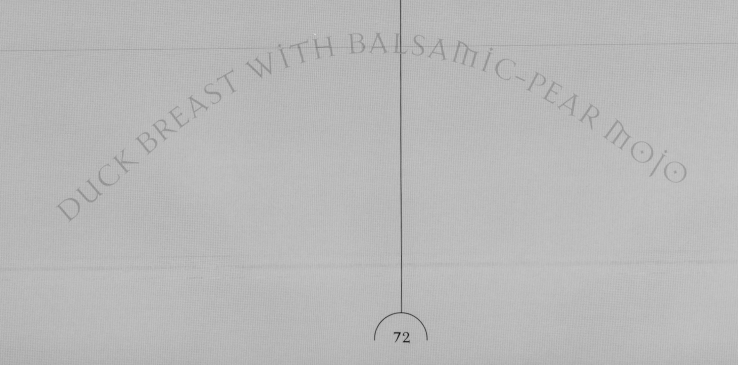

TURKEY STEAKS
WITH CRANBERRY MOJO

Serves 6

Turkey and cranberry sauce—a favorite combination! The cranberry mojo is one of the most vibrantly colored and tasty mojos I have ever enjoyed. The bits of cranberries offer a sweet and tart element that is offset nicely by the jalapeño and mustard oil. The lime juice supplies the citrus note that ties it all together. Boniato Mash with Ginger Butter (page 102) makes an excellent side dish.

6 (6-ounce) turkey steaks, cut 1/2-inch thick

MARINADE
3 tablespoons lemon zest
1/2 cup finely chopped fresh parsley
1/2 cup finely chopped fresh sage leaves
1 cup vegetable oil
Salt and freshly ground black pepper

CRANBERRY MOJO
1 quart cranberry juice
2 cups fresh or frozen cranberries (unthawed, if frozen)
1 medium red onion, finely chopped
1/2 cup finely chopped chives
2 jalapeños, seeded and minced
Juice of 5 limes
1/4 cup mustard oil
Salt and freshly ground black pepper

1. In a nonreactive dish, lay out the turkey steaks in a single layer. Combine the marinade ingredients and pour over the turkey. Marinate in the refrigerator for 4 hours.

2. To make the mojo, pour the cranberry juice into a nonreactive saucepan. Bring to a boil over high heat and reduce to a syrupy and glossy state. There should be about 1/2 cup of liquid left. Remove from the heat and set aside.

3. In a food processor, pulse the cranberries until a fine dice is achieved. Do not purée.

4. Transfer the cranberries to a mixing bowl and add the reduced cranberry juice, onion, chives, jalapeños, lime juice, mustard oil, and salt and pepper to taste. Mix well. Refrigerate.

5. Prepare a medium-hot fire in the grill.

6. Remove the turkey from the marinade and pat dry with paper towels. Place the turkey on the hot grate and grill for 5 to 6 minutes on each side. The turkey should be opaque in color and moist. Remove from the grill with tongs.

7. Transfer to serving plates and serve with mojo on the side.

TURKEY STEAKS WITH CRANBERRY MOJO

PAELLA CLASSICAL

Serves 6

Traditional paella comes from Valencia, the city in Spain from which it originates. The paella is always cooked on a wood-burning grill grate over indirect heat. The locals all argue about the type of wood to use— some prefer eucalyptus, for instance, which imparts a smoky flavor with minty overtones—but at home I cook it in my kettle grill over hardwood charcoal. The shape of the paella pan—shallow, wide, and with handles on each side—is important because it enables the rice to cook evenly without trapping too much moisture among the grains. To cook this paella indoors, just place your pan over medium-low heat on the stovetop and follow the directions as given.

3 tablespoons olive oil

1/2 cup finely diced white onion

8 ounces chorizo, cut into 1/4-inch rings

1 pound boneless, skinless chicken thighs, cut into 1/2-inch dice

8 ounces smoked ham, diced

4 cloves garlic, minced

2 cups Valencia or Arborio rice

2 cups white wine

2 (12-ounce) bottles beer

1 cup diced tomatoes

2 bay leaves

2 tablespoons saffron threads

1 tablespoon smoked Spanish paprika

6 cups lobster stock (page 176)

12 mussels, scrubbed and debearded

12 littleneck clams, washed and scrubbed

1 pound jumbo shrimp, peeled and deveined, tails left on

Salt and freshly ground black pepper

GARNISH

1 roasted red bell pepper (page 179), julienned

1 cup frozen sweet peas

2 tablespoons finely chopped parsley

1 cup diced marinated artichoke hearts

Saffron–Aji Amarillo Sauce (page 175), to serve

1. Prepare a hot fire in the grill.

2. Place the paella pan on the grate over the hottest area of the fire. Add the oil and the onion, chorizo, chicken, and ham and sauté for about 3 minutes, stirring with a spoon. Add the garlic and continue to sauté for 3 minutes. Add the rice and stir until all grains are coated with oil, about 2 minutes. Add the wine and beer and mix well. Add the tomatoes, bay leaves, saffron, and paprika. Keep stirring and let all the liquid evaporate, about 5 minutes.

3. Add 3 cups of the lobster stock to the pan and bring to a boil. Move the pan, if needed, to position it in the middle of the grate so the heat can circulate. Cover the grill to create an oven. Let simmer for 10 to 15 minutes.

4. Open the grill and add the mussels and clams to the rice, pushing each one in among the rice in a circular pattern: one clam, then one mussel, repeating the process until done. Then add the shrimp and the remaining 3 cups of stock. Cover the grill again and cook out the alcohol, about 5 minutes.

5. Open the grill and check to see if the mussels and clams are open. Season with salt and pepper, then scatter on top the roasted pepper, peas, parsley, and artichokes to garnish. Cover again and let cook for 3 more minutes.

6. Let rest for 5 minutes before serving with Saffron–Aji Amarillo Sauce on the side.

CORNISH GAME HENS
WITH HONEY-MUSTARD-GARLIC-CILANTRO GLAZE

Serves 6

There is nothing more pleasing than a perfectly grilled bone-in hen with a crispy skin and juicy tender-to-the-bone meat. But success is only achieved through attentive, slow, indirect grilling, so be patient! Serve these hens with Rum-Barbecued Black Beans (page 99).

HONEY-MUSTARD-GARLIC-CILANTRO GLAZE

3 tablespoons toasted celery seeds

3 tablespoons toasted black mustard seeds

2 cups honey

1/2 cup mustard oil

3 tablespoons Colman's mustard powder

6 cloves garlic, coarsely chopped

1/2 cup packed fresh cilantro leaves

3 tablespoons distilled white vinegar

2 tablespoons salt

3 tablespoons cracked black pepper

3 Cornish game hens, split in half lengthwise

1. To make the glaze, combine the celery and mustard seeds in a spice grinder and coarsely grind. Combine the ground seeds in a blender with the honey, mustard oil, mustard powder, garlic, cilantro, vinegar, salt, and pepper. Pulse on and off for about 15 seconds. Set aside.

2. Place the hens in a large, nonreactive glass dish or container. Add half the glaze, cover, and marinate in the refrigerator for at least 8 hours or overnight.

3. Prepare a medium fire in the grill with the coals piled on one side of the grill or with only one side of a gas grill fired up.

4. Place the hens skin side down on the grate opposite the heat source for indirect heat, cover the grill, and grill for 20 to 30 minutes, turning frequently and brushing with the reserved glaze, until the meat is tender and cooked through and the juices run clear.

5. Transfer hens to serving plates and serve.

CUBAN BURGERS

Serves 8

This is the Cuban version of the all-American hamburger. Instead of using ground beef, the patties are made from bulk chorizo. A Spanish sausage maker taught me to cook the paprika in oil before adding it to the chorizo because the spice is mixed in better when it's done this way. The patties and the crunchy potato sticks—the hybrid of potato chips and french fries—are piled on bread dressed with mustard. Using the right bread is very important. It should be soft, sweet Cuban bread. Portuguese sweet bread will also work. I sometimes substitute a piece of challah toast.

2 tablespoons olive oil

1 tablespoon smoked Spanish paprika or
 hot Hungarian paprika

1/2 teaspoon cayenne pepper

1 tablespoon ground pasilla chile

8 ounces pork loin, finely diced

1 pound pork butt, ground

1 tablespoon finely chopped garlic

1 teaspoon ground cumin

1 teaspoon ground coriander

2 tablespoons kosher salt

8 sweet rolls, split

American-style yellow mustard

2 (5-ounce) cans potato sticks

1. To make the patty mixture, heat the oil in a small pan over medium heat. Add the paprika, cayenne, and ground chile. Mix well and cook for about 2 minutes. Let cool.

2. In a large mixing bowl, combine the meat with the garlic, cumin, coriander, and salt. Add the cooled oil-and-spice mixture. With your hands, work in all ingredients until completely combined and of uniform color throughout. Shape the mixture into eight 5-ounce patties and refrigerate for 1 hour.

2. Prepare a medium-hot fire in the grill.

3. Lightly toast the rolls. Set aside.

4. Place the patties on the hot grate and grill for about 5 minutes per side. When done, the juices should run clear when the patties are pierced with a fork.

5. Spread mustard on the rolls and add a patty and a small handful of potato sticks. Top with the top half of the roll and serve.

CUBAN BURGERS

BUTTERFLIED LEG OF LAMB WITH PERUVIAN CHICHA DE JORA MARINADE

Serves 6 to 8

A few exotic ingredients give this lamb an authentic Peruvian taste. You'll probably have to shop for some of the ingredients through the mail (see Sources, page 183), but I promise it will be worth it. Chicha de jora *is Peruvian beer made from corn. It is used to flavor and tenderize meats in stews and marinades. Huacatay is Peruvian black mint. It has a wonderful grassy and minty aroma. Panca chiles are dried mild chiles with hints of tomato, raisins, and Tabasco. I serve the lamb with Peruvian Sarsa Salad (page 112) or Rice and Pea Salad (page 108).*

4- to 6-pound leg of lamb, boneless and butterflied

MARINADE

2 (12-ounce) bottles chicha de jora
  (substitute any amber beer)

1 white onion, coarsely diced

8 garlic cloves

3 tablespoons ground cumin

1/2 cup coarsely chopped cilantro

4 dried panca peppers with seeds
  (substitute ancho chiles)

1 (6-ounce) jar huacatay paste
  (substitute 1/2 cup chopped fresh mint)

Juice of 4 limes

Salt and freshly ground black pepper

1. Lay out the butterflied leg on a cutting board and trim away any excess fat or sinew. Make a few criss-cross slits into the meat with your knife and place in a nonreactive dish large enough to accommodate the lamb and marinade.

2. To prepare the marinade, combine the marinade ingredients in a blender and purée until smooth. Pour the marinade over the lamb and marinate in the refrigerator overnight.

3. Prepare a medium-hot fire in the grill with the coals piled to one side, or by firing only one side of a gas grill, for indirect grilling.

4. Lay the leg on the grate on the side opposite the coals and cover the grill. Grill, rotating and turning the lamb frequently, for about 1 1/2 hours, until the internal temperature registers 145°F on an instant-read thermometer.

5. Transfer the cooked lamb to a cutting board and let rest for 5 minutes before carving.

LEG OF LAMB

LAMB LOIN with Plantain and Pine Nut Crust

Serves 6

The plantains and pine nuts combined with the honey mustard give the loin an artful golden brown crust that has plenty of crunch. The radish slaw supplies a fierce clean finish that cuts the rich lamb. This recipe also works perfectly well with racks of lamb; just add a few more minutes to the cooking time.

PLANTAIN AND PINE NUT CRUST

1 quart oil, for frying chips

2 green plantains, peeled and thinly sliced on a mandoline

$^1/_2$ cup pine nuts, lightly toasted (page 179) and coarsely ground

3 tablespoons honey

3 tablespoons American-style yellow mustard

2 tablespoons finely chopped fresh rosemary

$^1/_4$ teaspoon cayenne pepper

Kosher salt

6 lamb loins, trimmed of sinew

Salt and freshly ground black pepper

Spicy Radish Slaw (page 109)

1. To prepare the crust, heat the oil to 350°F in a 3-quart saucepan. Carefully add the plantain slices, one by one, to the oil and fry for 2 to 3 minutes, until crisp and golden brown. Remove the chips from the oil with tongs and transfer to a plate lined with paper towels. When the chips have cooled, break them up with your hands. In a food processor, pulse to grind the chips into coarse crumbs; do not overprocess to a powder or the crust will lose its crunch. Place the plantain crumbs in a mixing bowl along with the ground pine nuts.

2. In a smaller separate bowl, combine the honey with the mustard. Add all but 3 teaspoonfuls to the crumb mixture. Then add the rosemary, cayenne, and salt and mix thoroughly. Set aside.

3. Prepare a medium-hot fire in the grill with all the coals piled on one side of the grill or by firing only one side of a gas grill.

4. Season the lamb with salt and pepper. Place on the hot grate directly over the hot coals and grill for 5 to 6 minutes, turning and rolling to sear in the juices. Move the lamb to a part of the grate that is over medium heat and continue to grill, turning and rolling to ensure even cooking, for 4 to 5 minutes longer, until the internal temperature registers 135°F on an instant-read thermometer (for medium-rare).

5. Remove the loins from the grill to a plate and spread with the reserved honey mustard. Then roll the lamb in the plantain crumb mixture, gently but firmly pressing the crumbs into place.

6. Return the lamb to a part of the grill that is not directly over the coals, cover the grill, and roast for another 3 to 4 minutes, until the crust browns slightly.

7. Transfer the meat to a cutting board and let rest before slicing. Place a scoop of the radish slaw in the center of the individual serving plates and arrange the meat slices around the slaw.

PORK CHOPS WITH OKRA, CORN, AND JALAPEÑO SALSA

Serves 6

Okra is one of the most underused vegetables around. Many people dislike it, claiming it is too slimy, but there's an answer for that: the night before you plan to prepare the salsa, cut the okra in 1/4-inch rounds. Scatter the rounds on a sheet pan and let them sit out at room temperature overnight in a cool, dry place. This step practically eliminates the sliminess of cooked okra. We like to use 1-inch-thick pork chops, but thinner ones work just as well; just be sure to decrease the cooking time.

6 pork chops, cut 1 inch thick

MARINADE
8 garlic cloves
1 white onion, chopped
2 bay leaves
2 tablespoons ground cumin
1/2 cup chopped fresh cilantro
1/2 cup distilled white vinegar
1 cup vegetable oil
Salt and freshly ground black pepper

OKRA, CORN, AND JALAPEÑO SALSA
2 tablespoons corn oil
2 cups fresh, sweet yellow corn kernels
2 pounds okra, stemmed and cut into 1/2-inch pieces
1/2 cup Pickled Jalapeño slices (page 177)
2 cups chopped fresh spinach
Salt and freshly ground black pepper

1. Place the chops in a nonreactive dish large enough to hold them in a single layer. Combine all the marinade ingredients in a blender and purée until smooth. Pour over the pork chops and marinate in the refrigerator for 8 hours.

2. To make the salsa, heat a large skillet over medium-high heat. Add the oil, then add the corn and toss for 2 minutes. Add the okra and continue to cook and toss for 2 minutes. Add the pickled jalapeños and chopped spinach and cook for 1 minute longer. Season to taste.

3. Prepare a medium fire in the grill.

4. Remove the chops from the marinade and pat dry with paper towels. Arrange the chops on the hot grate and grill for 6 to 8 minutes on each side until nicely browned, turning once. A thermometer inserted in the meaty part of the chops should register an internal temperature of 160°F.

5. Transfer the chops to serving plates, spoon salsa over each, and serve immediately.

QUICK PORK TENDERLOIN CHURRASCO WITH FAVA BEAN, POZOLE, AND POBLANO SALSA

Serves 6

Churrasco is Spanish for barbecued meat. These delicious strips of marinated pork tenderloin are perfect for the grill. They cook so quickly that you can prepare and marinate them in advance, then grill them once your guests have gathered and you are just ready to serve. Pair the tenderloin with most any other mojo or salsa in this book. This salsa is also great with grilled salmon, chicken, steak, and pork chops.

MARINADE

1 cup vegetable oil

1/2 cup annatto seeds

4 garlic cloves, chopped

2 rosemary sprigs, chopped

2 tablespoons fresh thyme leaves

Salt and freshly ground black pepper

3 pork tenderloins, trimmed of excess fat and silverskin

FAVA BEAN, POZOLE, AND POBLANO SALSA

2 cups fresh fava beans, removed from pods

2 cups white pozole (hominy)

4 ears corn, shucked and silks removed

4 poblano peppers, cut in 1/4-inch dice

6 shallots, finely minced

2 teaspoons chopped garlic

1/4 cup lemon juice

1/4 cup light olive oil

1/4 cup fresh cilantro leaves

2 tablespoons red wine vinegar

Salt and freshly ground black pepper

1. To prepare the marinade, set a saucepan over medium-high heat and add the oil and annatto seeds. Cook for 5 minutes, infusing the oil with the brick red color of the annatto. Remove from the heat and let cool to room temperature. When the oil is cooled, strain it and discard the seeds.

2. Combine the annatto oil with the garlic, rosemary, thyme, and salt and pepper in a blender and purée. Set aside.

3. Place a pork tenderloin on a cutting board and, with the tip of a sharp knife, starting at the top, cut into 4 equal strips lengthwise. Repeat with the remaining two tenderloins. Then place the pork between 2 pieces of plastic wrap and, with a meat mallet, pound out the pork to a thickness of 1/4 inch. Lay the pork in a single layer in a nonreactive rectangular container, cover with the marinade, and let it rest for at least 15 minutes.

4. To make the salsa, blanch the favas for approximately 3 minutes in a pot of salted boiling water. Drain, plunge into ice water to stop the cooking process, and drain again. Peel away the outer skin and discard. Place the beans in a bowl and set aside.

5. Drain the liquid from the pozole, rinse under cold running water, and blanch in boiling water for 3 minutes. Drain and add to the favas.

6. Over an open flame of a gas burner or grill, roast the peeled corn until lightly charred. With a sharp knife, cut down the sides of the corn to remove the kernels and add to the favas and pozole.

7. In a small bowl, prepare the dressing by combining the poblanos, shallots, garlic, lemon juice, olive oil, cilantro, and vinegar. Season with salt and pepper. Mix the poblano dressing with the pozole and favas and fold together. Set aside.

8. Prepare a medium-hot fire in the grill.

9. Remove the pork from the marinade, scrape away any excess marinade to prevent oil flare-ups, and lay out on the hot grate. Grill for just 1 or 2 minutes, then turn with a pair of tongs. Grill for another 2 minutes. The pork should be juicy and slightly pink.

10. Transfer the meat to a serving dish, spoon the salsa around, and serve.

PORK TENDERLOIN with Aji Amarillo–Pineapple Mojo

Serves 6

This is the most tender cut of pork, which makes it a natural for the grill's quick-searing char. The delicate flavor of the pork benefits from the piquant tang of the aji. I like my pork tenderloin a bit pink inside; if you do not, just leave it on the grill for 5 minutes longer. This mojo is terrific with grilled chicken breast, sliced turkey breast, and roasted duck. If you like it very hot, do not omit the chile seeds. Serve with rice and black beans on the side.

AJI AMARILLO–PINEAPPLE MOJO

4 dried aji amarillo (hot yellow peppers)

1 ripe pineapple, peeled and finely diced

1 medium-sized red onion, finely diced

1 yellow bell pepper, finely diced

1/2 cup finely sliced scallions, green part only

1/2 cup chopped cilantro

1/4 cup pineapple juice

Salt and freshly ground black pepper

2 teaspoons kosher salt

2 teaspoons black pepper

2 teaspoons ground ginger

2 teaspoons ground cardamom

2 teaspoons brown sugar

1/8 teaspoon cayenne

3 (10- to 12- ounce) pork tenderloins, trimmed clean of sinew

1. To make the mojo, soak the aji amarillo in warm water to cover for 1 hour. Drain the chiles, discard stems and seeds, and chop finely. Combine the chiles with the pineapple, onion, bell pepper, scallions, cilantro, and pineapple juice. Add salt and pepper to taste. Cover and refrigerate for up to 3 days.

2. In a small bowl, combine the salt, pepper, ginger, cardamom, brown sugar, and cayenne. Mix well. Season the pork with the spice mixture 2 to 4 hours before you plan to grill. Set aside in the refrigerator to marinate.

3. Prepare a medium-hot fire in the grill.

4. Lay out the seasoned tenderloins on the hot grate and grill for 5 minutes, turning often. Move the pork to a cooler area of the grill over medium coals and continue to grill, 8 to 10 minutes more, depending on the thickness of the meat. A thermometer inserted in the meat should register an internal temperature of 145°F.

5. Transfer the meat to a cutting board and let rest for 5 minutes. Then thinly slice the pork, arrange the slices on plates, and drizzle with the mojo.

BABY BACK RIBS
in Rain Forest Glaze

Serves 6 to 8

This is a unique example of the palate-pleasing result of combining sweet and tart tropical fruit with the fiery heat of the chiles. The ribs marinate for 8 hours, so be sure to allow the time. Always be patient while grilling ribs—a long, slow cooking time is what it takes to end up with a tender, fall-off-the-bone rack of ribs. Serve them with Grilled Hearts of Palm and Cherry Tomato Salad (page 120) and Grilled Smushed Potatoes (page 107).

4 racks baby pork ribs (3^1/$_2$ to 4 pounds)

MARINADE
1 onion, cut into pieces

4 garlic cloves

2 bay leaves, crumbled

^{1}/$_2$ cup coarsely chopped cilantro

2 tablespoons ground cumin

1 tablespoon crushed red pepper flakes

1 tablespoon salt

1 teaspoon freshly ground black pepper

1 cup distilled white vinegar

1 cup water

2 cups Rain Forest Glaze (page 156)

1. Prepare the ribs, removing the thin, papery membrane from the back of each rack by firmly gripping it with a towel and pulling. Place the ribs in a non-reactive roasting pan.

2. Combine all the marinade ingredients in a blender and purée until smooth and liquid. Pour it over the ribs, rubbing it onto both sides, and cover. Let the ribs marinate in the refrigerator for at least 8 hours, or overnight.

3. Prepare a medium-low fire in the grill.

4. Oil the grate. Remove the ribs from the marinade, place on the hot grate, and grill until the meat is tender, turning the meat every 10 minutes to prevent burning. This will take about 1 hour, until the meat has shrunk back from the ends of the bone. Use a spray bottle filled with water to extinguish flare-ups.

5. Using a brush, liberally apply glaze on both sides of the racks and continue to grill for an additional 15 minutes. Serve at once.

BABY BACK RIBS IN RAIN FOREST GLAZE

HAM STEAK with GRILLED PINEAPPLE-TOMATILLO SALSA

Serves 6

Ham and pineapple are a classic combination—the saltiness of the ham pairs beautifully with the sweetness of the pineapple and honey. The tomatillo adds the perfect acidic touch. Chipotle chiles supply a wonderful smoky heat to complete the dish. Because cured ham is always cooked, it does not require much cooking time. Serve with Crispy Yuca Hash Browns (page 109) or Fava Bean Purée (page 102).

GRILLED PINEAPPLE-TOMATILLO SALSA

15 tomatillos, peeled and washed

3 ($1/2$-inch-thick) slices pineapple

2 chipotle chiles in adobo

$1/4$ cup fresh cilantro leaves

3 tablespoons honey

1 onion, finely diced

$1/2$ teaspoon salt

6 ($1/4$-inch-thick) cured ham steaks

Salt and freshly ground black pepper

1. Prepare a medium fire in the grill.

2. Place the tomatillos on the hot grate and char on both sides for approximately 2 minutes per side. Remove from the grill and set aside. Grill the pineapple slices for about 3 minutes on both sides until grill marks appear. Set aside.

3. Combine the tomatillos, chipotle chiles, cilantro, and honey in a blender and pulse briefly to leave the mixture a bit chunky. Transfer to a bowl. Dice the grilled pineapple into $1/8$-inch pieces and add to the tomatillo mixture, along with the diced onion and salt. Place in the refrigerator to chill, or serve warm, if you prefer.

4. Season the ham on both sides with salt and pepper. Place the ham on the hot grate and grill for 4 to 5 minutes until well seared. Turn the ham and grill on the other side for 1 to 2 minutes, then spread with some of the salsa.

5. Transfer the ham to serving plates and serve.

HAM STEAK WITH GRILLED PINEAPPLE-TOMATILLO SALSA

STRIP STEAK with Horseradish-Parsley Mojo

Serves 6

Horseradish awakens the flavor of many cuts of beef, but this strip steak, with the Worcestershire background, stands up to the pungency of the mojo. Serve with Grilled Smushed Potatoes (page 107) or sliced ripe tomatoes. Any leftover mojo can be used to dress up a roast beef sandwich. It also complements salmon and oven-baked potatoes.

HORSERADISH-PARSLEY MOJO
4-inch piece fresh horseradish, peeled and finely grated

1 cup finely chopped flat-leaf parsley

1/2 cup finely chopped chives

6 shallots, finely chopped

Juice of 3 lemons

2 tablespoons white distilled vinegar

1/4 cup vegetable oil

1/2 teaspoon ground cumin

Salt and freshly ground black pepper

6 (8- to 10-ounce) strip steaks, cut 1 1/4 inches thick

3 tablespoons Worcestershire sauce

Kosher salt and freshly ground black pepper

Grilled Onion Rings (page 106), to serve

1. To prepare the mojo, thoroughly mix all the ingredients in a bowl, cover, and refrigerate.

2. At least 2 hours before you plan to grill, season both sides of the steaks with the Worcestershire sauce and salt and pepper, and place on a plate in the refrigerator.

3. Prepare a hot fire in the grill.

4. Lay the steaks out over the hottest portion of the grill and grill for 2 to 3 minutes per side to sear in the juices. Then move to a cooler spot over the coals (medium heat) and continue to grill for 3 to 4 minutes per side for medium-rare, until the meat is bright pink inside.

5. Mound some of the onions on each serving plate. Place the steaks over the onions on the plates and serve with mojo on the side.

STRIP STEAK WITH

HORSERADISH-PARSLEY MOJO

GRILLED PORTERHOUSE STEAK with Venezuelan Guasaca Sauce

Serves 6

I love to accept invitations to cook at different events around the world. It gives me a great opportunity to discover new flavors. When I was in Venezuela, I tasted a guasaca sauce—a traditional Venezuelan combination of mustard and avocados, which is a blend of ingredients I never would have thought worked together. When I described it to Andrew, he thought I was nuts! But as soon as he tasted it, he realized that it was one of the condiments that belongs at almost every barbecue. We hope you like it too. For a less formal, more portable way to serve this, split White Arepas (page 112), and fill with the steak and sauce to make sandwiches (as seen on opposite page).

GUASACA SAUCE

1 red onion, diced

5 cloves garlic

2 serrano chiles, with seeds, chopped

4 ripe Hass avocados, peeled and pitted

1/2 cup apple cider vinegar

1 cup pure olive oil

1 tablespoon Colman's mustard powder

1 tablespoon American-style yellow mustard

3 tablespoons chopped cilantro

2 tablespoons chopped parsley

1 tablespoon prepared horseradish

2 cups peeled and seeded ripe plum tomatoes

Salt

3 (2-pound) porterhouse steaks, cut about
   1 1/2 inches thick

Salt and freshly ground black pepper

1. To make the sauce, combine the onion, garlic, and chiles in a mortar and mash into paste with the pestle. In a blender, combine the avocados, vinegar, oil, and mustards and purée. Add the mashed garlic mixture and purée until smooth. Transfer to a bowl and fold in the cilantro, parsley, horseradish, and tomatoes. Add salt to taste and set aside.

2. Place the steaks on a plate and season generously with salt and pepper on both sides.

3. Prepare a medium-hot fire in the grill.

4. Place the steaks on the hot grate and grill to the desired doneness, about 5 to 8 minutes on each side for medium-rare.

5. Transfer to a serving dish and spread the sauce on the steaks.

PORTERHOUSE STEAK WITH

VENEZUELAN GUASACA SAUCE

[SERVED ON AREPAS]

NICARAGUAN-STYLE CHURRASCO

Serves 6 to 8

Churrasco is a traditional Argentinean dish made with skirt steak, a flavorful but fairly tough piece of meat cut from the beef skirt. The cut was invented by a famous steakhouse in Nicaragua, called Los Ranchos, and the objective is to imitate the look of a long strip of steak that, when cooked, is tender enough to be cut with a fork. I make my version with beef tenderloin—it's not as economical as using skirt steak, but it elevates a humble dish to company food.

PARSLEY CHIMICHURRI

6 cloves garlic

3 bay leaves

2 jalapeño chiles, with seeds, coarsely chopped

1 1/2 tablespoons salt

1/2 cup finely minced fresh curly parsley

1/2 cup fresh finely minced flat-leaf parsley

1/4 cup fresh finely minced oregano

1/4 cup distilled white vinegar

1/3 cup extra virgin olive oil

1 (5-pound) whole beef tenderloin

Salt and freshly ground black pepper

1. To make the chimichurri, combine the garlic, bay leaves, jalapeños, and salt in a mortar and mash with a pestle until a smooth paste is formed (or you can purée with a small amount of vinegar in a blender). Transfer to a mixing bowl and add the parsleys and oregano. Whisk in the vinegar and olive oil until well combined. Set aside.

2. Prepare a medium-hot fire in the grill.

3. Trim the meat and remove any silverskin. Cut into 2 1/2-inch-thick rounds. Take the boning knife and cut in a circular motion so each round becomes one flat, long strip. Then, with a butcher's mallet, pound the meat lightly. Season each strip generously with salt and pepper on each side.

4. Lightly oil the grate and place the meat on the grate. Grill for 3 minutes on each side for medium-rare.

5. Transfer the meat to a serving plate. Serve with the chimichurri on the side.

BEEF TENDERLOIN with Shiitake Mushroom Mojo

Serves 6

Truly a meat and mushroom lover's delight! Here's a tender filet mignon, enhanced with the smokiness of the grill, combined with earthy mushrooms, and finally cut by the acidic edge of the lemon. A wedge of Crispy Yuca Hash Browns (page 109) lends the perfect textural touch.

SHIITAKE MUSHROOM MOJO

2 tablespoons extra virgin olive oil

2 cups fresh shiitake mushrooms, stems removed and caps cut into $1/4$-inch dice

2 tablespoons finely chopped shallots

3 cloves garlic, finely chopped

$1/4$ cup dry white wine or juice of 2 lemons

1 cup thinly sliced scallions, green and white parts

1 tablespoon fresh thyme leaves

1 tablespoon chopped fresh cilantro, chopped

Juice of 2 lemons

2 tablespoons white truffle oil

Salt and freshly ground black pepper

3-pound center-cut beef tenderloin

4 tablespoons oil

Salt and freshly ground black pepper

1. To make the mojo, heat the oil over medium heat in a small saucepan. Add the mushrooms, shallots, and garlic and sauté for 5 minutes. Add the wine to the pan and cook for 2 more minutes. Transfer to a bowl and add the scallions, thyme, cilantro, lemon juice, and truffle oil. Mix well and season with salt and pepper. Set aside.

2. Place the beef on a cutting board and, with a sharp knife, cut into six 8-ounce portions.

3. Prepare a medium-hot fire in the grill.

4. Lightly brush the steaks with oil and season with salt and pepper. Arrange the steaks on the hot grate and grill to the desired doneness, about 5 to 6 minutes per side for medium-rare.

5. Transfer to a serving dish and spoon some mojo over each steak. Serve immediately.

SMOKED FRONTIER BUFFALO RIB EYE
WITH GRILLED PLANTAINS

Serves 6

Talk about an explosion of flavors—just about every-one does after they taste this dish! First, it hits you with an alluring smokiness. Next, you're tickled with the sweet heat of the spice, which brings you to the heart of the matter—the meat. Perfectly juicy inside a slightly charred, crispy exterior. But that's not all. You still have the rich, intensely luxurious plantains to savor. Then, finally, your palate is cleansed by the balsamic glaze on the plantains. For just the right flavor you will need to use a charcoal (not gas) fire and pre-soaked wood for smoking (oak, hickory, or mesquite, for example). If buffalo rib eye isn't available, simply substitute beef rib eye.

5-pound bone-in buffalo rib eye rack, trimmed
1¹/₂ cups Barbecue Spice Rub (page 151)
Plantains with Balsamic-Basil Glaze (page 107)

1. Prepare a medium-hot fire in the grill and presoak wood chips.

2. Season the meat liberally with the spice mixture. When the briquettes are gray with ash, toss some wood chips directly over them. Arrange the rib eye on the hot grate, cover the grill to retain the smoke, and grill for 10 to 15 minutes on each side for medium-rare.

3. Transfer the rib eye to a chopping block and let rest for 5 minutes before slicing.

4. Transfer to serving plates and serve with plantains.

SIDES

RUM-BARBECUED BLACK BEANS

Serves 8 to 10

This version of black beans is made for the home cook, using canned black beans. It's a trick my mother taught me. I like to make the beans the night before and just warm them up on the side of the grill.

6 ounces smoked bacon, finely diced

1 cup diced yellow onion

4 cloves garlic, finely chopped

6 cachucha chiles, finely chopped

2 jalapeño chiles, finely chopped

8 ounces chorizo, diced

$^1/_2$ cup ketchup

$^1/_4$ cup American-style yellow mustard

1 teaspoon Colman's mustard powder

$^1/_2$ teaspoon ground ginger

$^1/_2$ cup dark rum

2 tablespoons brown sugar

$^1/_2$ cup light molasses

1 tablespoon Tabasco sauce

2 tablespoons Worcestershire sauce

3 (15-ounce) cans black beans, drained

Salt

1. In a large saucepan over medium heat, cook the bacon for 7 to 8 minutes, stirring continuously with a wooden spoon, until the bacon is brown and crispy. Add the onion, garlic, cachucha chiles, and jalapeños. Lower the heat and continue to cook for 5 minutes, until the onions become translucent. Add the chorizo, ketchup, mustard, mustard powder, ginger, rum, brown sugar, molasses, Tabasco, and Worcestershire sauce. Increase the heat and bring to a boil; then reduce to a simmer.

2. Drain the beans, rinse gently under cold running water, drain again, add them to the sauce, and stir well. Continue to simmer for about 1 hour. Season with salt. Turn off the heat and let the beans cool.

3. Reheat again when you are ready to serve.

RUM-BARBECUED BLACK BEANS

GRILLED ASPARAGUS
WITH CRAB MAYONNAISE

Serves 6 to 8

This is an especially simple dish to prepare and serve. It works well as an appetizer or as an accompaniment to fish, chicken, or veal.

1 pound asparagus

2 tablespoons oil

Salt and freshly ground black pepper

1 cup mayonnaise

Zest and juice of 3 lemons

2 tablespoons adobo sauce
  (from canned chipotles in adobo)

1 pound Alaskan crabmeat, picked clean of shells

1/4 cup finely sliced chives

1/2 cup finely diced red onion

2 tablespoons julienned cilantro

4 red jalapeños, stemmed, seeded, and diced

1. Blanch the asparagus in boiling salted water for 4 to 6 minutes, depending on the thickness of the stalks. Plunge into ice water to stop the cooking. Drain. Peel away the tough outer skin.

2. Prepare a medium-low fire in the grill.

3. In a bowl, toss the asparagus with oil and season with salt and pepper. Arrange the asparagus crosswise on the hot grate to prevent them from falling through. Grill for 1 to 2 minutes on both sides, until lightly charred, and transfer to a serving dish.

4. In another bowl, combine the mayonnaise with the lemon zest and juice, adobo sauce, and salt and pepper to taste. Mix well. Gently fold in the crabmeat, chives, red onion, cilantro, and jalapeños.

5. Spoon the crab mayonnaise over the asparagus and serve.

GRILLED ASPARAGUS WITH CRAB MAYO

FAVA BEAN PURÉE

Serves 8

I like tender, sweet fresh fava beans, but Andrew prefers dried yellow favas for their comforting and earthy quality. So we compromised and used both!

2 cups dried peeled favas, soaked in water overnight
¹/4 cup butter or extra virgin olive oil
Kosher salt and freshly ground black pepper
1 cup shelled fresh favas

1. Place the soaked fava beans in a saucepan with enough water to cover and bring to a boil. Lower the heat and simmer for 30 to 45 minutes, or until the beans are fork tender. Drain the beans, place in a bowl, and mash with butter or oil. Season with salt and pepper and set aside.

2. In another saucepan, blanch the fresh favas in boiling salted water for 3 to 4 minutes. Drain, plunge into ice water to stop the cooking, and drain again. Remove the thin outer peel by pinching off the top portion of the peel and gently squeezing the bean out.

3. Fold the blanched favas into the purée and serve immediately.

BONIATO MASH
WITH GINGER BUTTER

Serves 6

Boniato is a variety of sweet potato. It has a thick, light yellow skin and pale yellow, mealy flesh that is less sweet than regular sweet potatoes. Boniato combined with ginger is a flavor combination I never tire of— chilled boniato and ginger soup, gingered boniato chips, or buñuelos of boniato with ginger syrup are just a few of the other dishes I make with them. Try this recipe for a Thanksgiving twist on ordinary sweet potatoes. Your turkey and guests will definitely appreciate it. Also, try this tasty "trimming" with grilled salmon, chicken breast, and pork tenderloin.

2 pounds boniatos (about 6 small ones)
2 teaspoons salt
1-inch piece fresh ginger, peeled and grated
6 tablespoons unsalted butter
¹/2 cup milk

1. Peel the boniatos and cut into large chunks. Place in a pot with ¹/2 teaspoon salt and cover with water. Bring to a boil and cook for about 20 minutes or until easily pierced with a fork. Drain boniatos, shake the pot over medium heat to let all excess moisture evaporate, and transfer boniatos to a bowl.

2. Add the ginger pulp and juice to the bowl, discarding any tough fibers. Mash the boniatos with a potato masher, adding the butter, milk, and the remaining 1¹/2 teaspoons salt as you make a smooth purée. Serve warm.

GRILLED CARROT PURÉE
FLAVORED WITH SAFFRON AND MAPLE SYRUP

Serves 6

This purée goes well with poultry and pork. Choose carrots that are similar in size, to guarantee even cooking.

6 cups water

2 pounds carrots, peeled

1 large pinch saffron threads

1 teaspoon salt

4 tablespoons butter

Salt and freshly ground black pepper

1/4 cup pure maple syrup

1. In a medium-size saucepan, combine the water, carrots, saffron, and 1 teaspoon salt. Bring to a boil and cook the carrots for 12 to 15 minutes, or until the carrots are tender but firm. You do not want them to break or fall apart.

2. Transfer the whole, blanched carrots to a bowl, gently toss with 1 tablespoon of the butter to coat on all sides, and season with salt and pepper.

3. Prepare a medium fire in the grill.

4. Arrange the carrots crosswise on the hot grate and grill until the carrots have definite and dark grill markings, about 5 minutes.

5. Return the carrots to the bowl and add maple syrup and the remaining 3 tablespoons butter. Mash the carrots, but leave a bit chunky, if you wish. Serve warm.

BACON-WRAPPED CAULIFLOWER WITH
RED CHILE OIL AND LEMON

Serves 6

If you think cauliflower tastes bland, you will be pleasantly surprised how delicious it can be when it's prepared on the grill instead of the stovetop. With the smoky flavor of the grill and bacon, along with the lift the cauliflower gets from the chile oil and lemon juice, it practically tastes like a whole different vegetable.

2 teaspoons salt

1 whole cauliflower, trimmed of outer leaves

6 strips thick-sliced bacon

Salt and freshly ground black pepper

1/4 cup Red Chile Oil (page 150)

Juice of 1 lemon

1. In a medium-size saucepan, bring 8 cups water to a boil with 2 teaspoons of salt. Add the cauliflower and blanch for 4 to 5 minutes. Drain, plunge into ice water to stop the cooking process, and drain again. The cauliflower should still be firm and intact.

2. Using toothpicks, secure the bacon slices to the cauliflower in a crisscross fashion, from the bottom of one end to the bottom on the opposite side.

3. Prepare a medium-hot fire in the grill with all the coals piled on one side or only one side of a gas grill fired for indirect heat.

4. Place the cauliflower right side up on the grate opposite the heat source, cover the grill, and roast for 6 to 7 minutes. Turn the cauliflower to crisp the bacon on the other side for 3 to 4 minutes.

5. Place the cauliflower on a cutting board and, with a heavy sharp knife, cut the vegetable into 8 to 10 wedges. Transfer to a serving dish, season with salt and pepper, and drizzle with red chile oil and lemon juice.

GRILLED CORN ON THE COB
WITH CHIPOTLE MAYO

Serves 6

My good friend Stephen Schimoler, who owns a company called Chef Stuff, served us this vegetable at a party at his house, and I fell in love with it!

6 ears corn, shucked

3 tablespoons mayonnaise

3 tablespoons puréed chipotles in adobo sauce

Pinch salt

1. Prepare a medium-low fire in the grill.

2. Bring a large pot of water to a boil, add the corn, and cook for 3 minutes.

3. Meanwhile, mix together the mayonnaise, chipotle purée, and salt. Remove the corn from the hot water and, with a paintbrush, coat the corn with the mayonnaise.

4. Place on the hot grate and grill, turning often, until the kernels are golden brown, about 5 minutes.

5. Give the corn a final brush with the mayonnaise and serve at once.

MARINATED QUESO BLANCO

Serves 6

Find a little room on your plate for this go-with-anything side dish. Serve it over sliced tomatoes or with crisp fried plantains. As a variation, add blanched broccoli or green beans. A grilled and diced chicken breast can also be tossed in.

16 ounces queso blanco (preferably El Viajero brand), cut into 1/4-inch dice

2 roasted red bell peppers (page 179), diced

1 tablespoon chopped garlic

1 tablespoon chopped red onion

1 tablespoon chopped cilantro

1 tablespoon chopped chives

1 tablespoon chopped parsley

1 tablespoon crushed red pepper flakes

1/4 cup distilled white vinegar

6 tablespoons olive oil

1 teaspoon salt

1/2 teaspoon freshly ground black pepper

1. Combine all ingredients in a bowl and toss well.

2. This dish is best enjoyed at room temperature, but keep any unused portion refrigerated for up to 3 days.

CORN ON THE COB

GRILLED MUSHROOM AND MALANGA SALAD

Serves 6

Everywhere in Latin America, you will find a long, knobby, starchy tuber that is called malanga (or taro or yautia). By any name, it is recognizable by its thin, shaggy brown skin. The crispy beige, yellow, or red flesh has a sweet, nutty flavor. For the best results, have all the components for the salad ready and warm at the time of assembly. (This ensures that the earthy flavor of the mushroom and malanga will be at their best when served.) This extraordinary salad is superb with any grilled steak.

1 pound large shiitake mushroom caps

3 portobello mushrooms

1 pound button mushrooms

1/4 cup balsamic vinegar

2 tablespoons olive oil

1 tablespoon minced garlic

2 tablespoons fresh thyme leaves

1 tablespoon chopped fresh rosemary leaves

1/2 cup thinly sliced shallots

1/2 cup thinly sliced scallions, white and green parts

Salt and freshly ground black pepper

2 1/2 pounds malanga, peeled and sliced 1/2 inch thick

11 ounces fresh chèvre (goat cheese), crumbled

1/2 cup white truffle oil

2 cups vegetable oil, for frying

12 round slices ripe, red beefsteak tomatoes

1. In a large bowl, combine the mushrooms. Add the vinegar, olive oil, garlic, thyme, rosemary, shallots, scallions, and salt and pepper. Marinate for 1 hour.

2. Prepare a hot fire in the grill.

3. Remove the mushrooms from the marinade and reserve the marinade for later. Place a vegetable/fish grill rack on the grate. Place the mushrooms on the rack and grill for 2 to 3 minutes per side. The portobellos may require a bit more time on the grill. When the mushrooms are cooked, transfer to a plate and let cool. Cut them into 1/2-inch pieces and transfer them with any accumulated juices to the reserved balsamic marinade. Toss to coat.

4. To prepare malanga, cube 2 pounds and set the remaining 1/2 pound aside. Add the 2 pounds cubed malanga to a large pot of boiling salted water and boil for 8 to 10 minutes, until the malanga is tender but still holds its shape. Drain, plunge into ice water to stop the cooking, and drain again. Transfer to the bowl with the mushrooms. Add the goat cheese and truffle oil and gently toss to mix all ingredients.

5. To prepare the remaining 1/2 pound malanga, slice very thin using a mandoline, any vegetable slicer, or box grater. Cut the slices crosswise into fine strips with a sharp knife.

6. In a medium-size sauté pan, heat the oil to 350°F and fry the malanga until golden brown and crisp. Transfer to paper towels to drain.

7. To serve, spoon the mushroom salad over the tomato slices and sprinkle with the fried malanga.

GRILLED ONION RINGS

Serves 8

The onions can be prepared early and kept warm until ready to serve over steaks, fish, or just about anything.

1/4 cup minced fresh thyme

2 tablespoons minced rosemary leaves

1/4 cup red wine vinegar

1/4 cup olive oil

Salt and freshly ground black pepper

4 Spanish onions, peeled and cut into 1/2-inch slices

6 red Bermuda onions, peeled and cut into 1/2-inch slices

1. In a bowl, combine the thyme, rosemary, vinegar, oil, and salt and pepper and mix well. Arrange the onions in a single layer in a large container. Pour the marinade over and set aside for at least 1 hour, but no more than 4 hours, to marinate.

2. Prepare a medium-hot fire in the grill, with the coals piled on one side or only one side of the gas grill fired up.

3. Arrange the onion slices on the grate on the side opposite the heat source. Grill for 2 to 3 minutes on each side, using tongs to turn the onions. Serve warm.

GRILLED SMUSHED POTATOES

Serves 6

For grill gatherings, I like to borrow from the tasting menu way of serving, which we do at the restaurant. These potatoes make a perfect base for such tiny tastings. For example, I might arrange one grilled shrimp, a few slices of beef tenderloin, or a small piece of grilled fish atop one of the flattened potatoes and then garnish it with a sauce or salsa to create a miniature meal. Choose small round Yukon Golds, Red Bliss, or, my favorite, Peruvian Purple potatoes.

2 pounds small red, purple, or gold potatoes, unpeeled

2 teaspoons salt plus additional, for seasoning

$^1/_4$ cup butter

Freshly ground black pepper

1. In a medium-size saucepan, combine the potatoes with 10 cups water and the 2 teaspoons salt. Bring to a boil and boil for about 10 minutes, until the potatoes are easily pierced with a skewer. Be careful not to overcook. Drain the potatoes and set aside to cool.

2. When the potatoes are cool enough to handle, place 1 potato on a flat surface and, with the palm of your hand, smush it to form a $^1/_2$-inch-thick disk. Repeat with the remaining potatoes.

3. Prepare a medium fire in the grill.

4. When you are ready to serve, oil the grill grate and simply place the potatoes on the grill to reheat on both sides.

5. Transfer to a serving plate. Spread butter over the potatoes and season with salt and pepper.

PLANTAINS
WITH BALSAMIC-BASIL GLAZE

Serves 8

No backyard barbecue is complete at the Rodriguez household without some of these plantains. Once you have tried them, you'll feel the same way. The important factor here is to choose plantains that are neither too green nor too ripe. Only the yellow and sweet but firm ones will do, the ones that are called "pinton."

$^1/_2$ cup balsamic vinegar

1 cup unsalted butter, at room temperature

3 tablespoons honey

2 tablespoons chopped fresh basil

1 teaspoon salt

4 sweet yellow plantains, unpeeled

1. Prepare a medium fire in the grill.

2. In a small saucepan over high heat, boil the vinegar to reduce its volume to $^1/_4$ cup.

3. In a small bowl, combine the reduced vinegar with the butter, honey, basil, and salt. Using a whisk, vigorously whip the butter until smooth and all ingredients are blended.

4. With a paring knife, make a shallow cut into the curved side of each plantain lengthwise, from end to end. Repeat the process, making the second cut $^1/_2$ inch away from the first. Remove the $^1/_2$-inch piece of peel, then, using your fingers, gently pry away the peel from the sides of each plantain. Next, take some balsamic butter and spread generously over the entire inside of each plantain, leaving the peel on the outside intact.

5. Place the plantains on the outer perimeter of the grill to receive indirect heat. Grill for about 1 hour, basting with the remaining balsamic butter.

6. To serve, place whole plantains on a serving plate. Using a soup spoon, scoop out spoonfuls of the plantain flesh to serve individual portions.

RICE AND PEA SALAD

Serves 6

Rice and peas are a combo found in many dishes, including paella and risotto. This version is a suitable side dish for many grilled meats and fish. Fresh English peas are available in the spring and summer and should be used whenever possible. A small amount of work is required to shell them, but the end result is well worth the time.

1 cup fresh shelled peas

2 cups cooked white rice

1/2 cup diced red bell pepper

1/4 cup chopped scallions, green parts only

4 cloves garlic

2 tablespoons distilled white vinegar

1 whole egg

1 egg yolk

1/2 cup olive oil

Salt and freshly ground black pepper

1. Blanch the peas in boiling salted water for 5 minutes. Drain, plunge into ice water to stop the cooking, and drain again.

2. In a mixing bowl toss together the peas, rice, bell pepper, and scallions.

3. Combine the garlic, vinegar, egg, and egg yolk in a blender and purée. With the blender running, add the oil in a slow steady stream to emulsify. Season with salt and pepper.

4. Pour the dressing over the rice and mix thoroughly. Refrigerate until ready to serve.

STICKY ORANGE- AND CHIPOTLE-GLAZED SWEET POTATOES

PICTURED ON PAGES 96–97

Serves 6

This one could be called "Grandma's Candied Yams Meet the Latin Grill." These potatoes are pure heaven with any grilled chicken dish.

3 sweet potatoes, peeled and sliced 1/2 inch thick

2 teaspoons salt

1 (5-ounce) can frozen orange juice concentrate

1/4 cup unsalted butter

3 tablespoons adobo sauce (from canned chipotles in adobo)

1 tablespoon chopped fresh cilantro (optional)

1. Place the sweet potatoes in a pot with water and 1 teaspoon salt. Bring to a boil, lower to a simmer, and gently cook the potatoes for 4 to 5 minutes, until partially cooked, making sure not to break them. Drain, plunge the potatoes in ice water to stop the cooking, and drain again.

2. Meanwhile, in a small saucepan over low heat, combine the orange juice concentrate, butter, chipotle sauce, and the remaining 1 teaspoon salt and keep stirring until the butter is melted. Remove from the heat and fold in the cilantro.

3. Spread a little glaze on each potato slice.

4. Prepare a medium fire in the grill with the coals all piled on one side, or with only one side of a gas grill fired up.

5. Arrange the slices on the hot grate opposite the heat source. Grill the potato slices for 2 to 3 minutes on each side, occasionally brushing on more glaze. With tongs or a spatula, carefully transfer to a serving dish.

6. Serve warm.

SPICY RADISH SLAW

Serves 6

This cool, spicy, and refreshing slaw can be made a day in advance. It is an exceptional side dish for just about every food.

12 red radishes, cut into matchstick pieces

1 small daikon radish

4 ounces jicama, julienned

4 ounces daikon radish sprouts

1 medium red onion, thinly sliced

1/4 cup mustard oil (available where Indian foods are sold)

Juice of 3 limes

3 tablespoons chopped fresh parsley

2 teaspoons salt

1/2 cup thinly sliced chives

1. Mix together all the ingredients.

2. Refrigerate before serving.

CRISPY YUCA HASH BROWNS

Serves 6

These Nuevo Latino–style hash browns are deliciously crisp, and the nutty flavor of the yuca seems to be magnified by the cooking process. Serve with any grilled meat. Even a simple mixed green salad would be supported nicely by this crunchy yuca side dish.

2 pounds yuca, peeled

1 small white onion, diced

1/4 cup vegetable oil

Salt and freshly ground black pepper

1. On the coarse side of a hand-held box grater, shred the yuca. Place in a bowl with the diced onion and mix well.

2. Heat the oil in a nonstick 10-inch sauté pan over medium-high heat. Carefully place the shredded yuca and onion mixture in the hot pan and flatten out with a spatula. Cook for 3 to 4 minutes on one side, until the bottom has a golden brown crust. Flip with a spatula and cook an additional 3 to 4 minutes.

3. Transfer to a plate lined with a paper towel to absorb any excess oil. Season with salt and pepper. Cut into quarters and serve hot.

PANECITOS DE AGUA
(INDIVIDUAL WATER BREAD LOAVES)

Makes 4 individual loaves

The following recipe is a versatile, easy, and delicious bread that my assistant Hortensia used to make with her students in the cooking classes she taught at the New School. Since the bread can be made almost at a moment's notice, she adapted it for my cooking classes. The dough has only one proofing, and so the students are able to enjoy it when they sit down to sample the rest of the meal they had learned to prepare in the class. You can personalize the recipe by adding any combination of herbs or spices along with the flour. The dough can also be divided in half, to make 2 large loaves. Just increase the baking time to 60 minutes.

2 tablespoons active dry yeast

$3^{1}/_{2}$ cups warm water

$7^{1}/_{2}$ to 8 cups all-purpose flour

$^{1}/_{3}$ cup sugar

1 tablespoon salt

$^{1}/_{4}$ cup cornmeal, to sprinkle on baking sheet

GLAZE

$^{2}/_{3}$ cup water

2 teaspoons cornstarch

1. Dissolve the yeast in $^{1}/_{2}$ cup of the warm water and let stand until mixture is foamy, about 10 minutes. Slowly add 5 cups of flour, the remaining 3 cups water, the sugar, and salt, and mix thoroughly. Mix in the remaining $2^{1}/_{2}$ to 3 cups flour, until a slightly sticky dough forms. Turn out onto a lightly floured board and knead the dough until it is smooth and elastic, 5 to 7 minutes, adding more flour only as needed.

2. Oil a large bowl, add the dough, and turn it to coat. Cover lightly with plastic wrap and let it rise in a warm place until doubled, about 40 minutes.

3. While the dough is proofing, combine the glaze ingredients in a small saucepan and cook over medium heat just until bubbly. Set aside.

4. When the dough has risen to double its original size, punch it down, turn it out on a lightly floured work surface, and divide into 4 equal pieces. Briefly knead each piece and shape into a ball. Place all 4 pieces on a baking sheet that has been sprinkled with cornmeal. With a sharp knife, make $^{1}/_{4}$- to $^{1}/_{2}$-inch deep slashes on top of each loaf and brush with the glaze. Place the baking sheet in a *cold* oven. This is important. As the oven temperature rises, so will the dough.

5. Set the temperature at 350° and bake for about 40 minutes, until the loaves are nicely browned and sound hollow when tapped on the bottom. While baking, spray the loaves twice with cold water. Transfer the loaves to a cooling rack.

6. Serve warm or at room temperature.

PANECITOS DE AGUA

PERUVIAN SARSA SALAD

Serves 6

Peru's version of a chopped salad is robustly flavored with a lot of texture. You see it in many restaurants, as well as in refrigerated cases in airports. There are many versions, but radish, black mint, onions, and cheese are consistently seen. Serve with any grilled meats in this book, especially lamb. To make ahead, combine all the ingredients but do not dress with the oil and lemon juice.

1/2 cup fresh fava beans

1/2 cup red radish slices

1/2 cup mote (large white corn from Peru) kernels (substitute whole hominy)

1/4 cup crumbled feta cheese

1 red onion, thinly sliced

1/4 cup fresh huacatay (Peruvian black mint) leaves, loosely packed (substitite fresh mint)

1/4 cup diced roasted red bell pepper (page 179)

3 tablespoons garlic oil

2 tablespoons freshly squeezed lemon juice

Salt and freshly ground black pepper

1. Blanch the favas in a pot of salted boiling water for 3 to 4 minutes. Drain, plunge into ice water to stop the cooking, and drain again. Remove the thin outer peel by pinching off the top portion of the peel and gently squeezing the bean out. Place the beans in a large bowl.

2. Add the radishes, mote kernels, cheese, onion, huacatay, and roasted red pepper. Gently, but thoroughly, toss to mix. Add the garlic oil and lemon juice and season with salt and pepper.

3. Serve at once.

WHITE AREPAS

Makes 12 large or 24 small pancakes

Arepas are hearty pancakes from Colombia and Venezuela that are made with flour ground from a very starchy cooked corn. There's no substitute for the white corn arepa flour, but you can find it at any Latin market. Arepas cook quickly on a griddle. They can also be made directly on a grill.

1 cup white corn arepa flour

1/2 teaspoon salt

1 cup warm water

1/2 cup butter, at room temperature

6 tablespoons shredded mozzarella cheese

1. In a large bowl, combine the flour and salt with the warm water. Slowly blend in the butter and cheese.

2. Using a 1 1/2- or 3-inch ring mold, form the mixture into about 12 large or 24 small patties. Stack them on a lightly greased baking sheet with parchment paper between the layers. Refrigerate for 30 minutes.

3. Heat a lightly oiled griddle over medium-low heat or clean the grill with a wire brush and brush with oil to prevent sticking. Arrange the arepas on the hot surface and cook for 3 to 4 minutes on each side, turning once. Serve hot.

AREPAS

PUMPKIN SEED BOLLOS

Makes 12 rolls

Here is a simple roll with a Guatemalan twist that is great for breakfast or hamburgers.

1/3 cup finely chopped pumpkin seeds, toasted
1 tablespoon active dry yeast
1 1/2 cups warm water
1 tablespoon sugar
1 tablespoon pumpkin seed oil
1 1/2 teaspoons salt
3 to 3 1/2 cups all purpose flour

GLAZE
1/3 cup water
1 teaspoon cornstarch

1. Preheat the oven to 350°F.

2. Place the pumpkin seeds in a small dry sauté pan over medium heat. Shake the pan for a few minutes so that the seeds do not burn. They will crackle, pop, and turn light brown. Cool, chop coarsely, and set aside.

3. Dissolve the yeast in 1/2 cup of the warm water and let rest for 10 minutes.

4. Combine the remaining 1 cup water, sugar, oil, and salt. Stir in about 2 cups of the flour, as well as the pumpkin seeds. Add the yeast mixture and slowly stir in another 1 cup flour. Turn out onto a floured surface and keep on kneading in just enough of the remaining 1/2 cup flour until you have a firm but sticky dough.

5. Place the dough in a lightly oiled bowl and turn over. Cover the bowl with plastic wrap and let the dough rise until doubled.

6. Punch the dough down, place on a floured surface, and knead until it feels smooth and elastic. Pinch off 2-ounce pieces and shape each one into a smooth ball. Place on a baking sheet covered with parchment, and with a sharp knife make a cut about 1/4 to 1/2 inch deep on top of each ball. Cover and let rise in a warm place until nearly doubled.

7. To make the glaze, combine the water and cornstarch, and cook over medium heat just until it bubbles. Slightly cool the mixture and, with a soft brush, evenly brush on each bollo.

8. Bake the rolls in the preheated oven for about 20 to 25 minutes.

PUMPKIN

SEED

BOLLOS

NO-RISE GRILLED CHICAMA FLATBREADS

Makes 6

We serve this grilled bread to our customers plain and sprinkled with sesame seeds, and they drizzle it with chimichurri. Whenever there is a bit of dough left, we whip up a tasty topping—like thin-sliced, cooked blue potatoes, caramelized onions, queso blanco, olives, and mushrooms. We can't wait for the bread to come off the grill and usually fight each other for the pieces! Be sure to prepare a medium-low fire in the grill when you start to make the dough.

1 tablespoon active dry yeast

2 cups warm water

1 tablespoon light corn syrup or honey

4 cups all-purpose flour

1 1/2 teaspoons salt

Olive oil, for brushing

Sesame seeds (optional)

Fresh rosemary, minced (optional)

1. Prepare a medium-low fire in the grill.

2. In a medium bowl, combine the yeast with the water and corn syrup and let rest for 10 minutes, until foamy. Stir in about 3 1/2 cups of the flour and add the salt. Add the remaining 1/2 cup flour a few tablespoons at a time, adding it only until you have a sticky dough. Transfer the dough to a floured surface and divide into 6 equal portions.

3. Flour your hands generously and, with your fingertips, press and pull each portion until it is an oval about 5 inches wide and 7 inches long. Dust each oval lightly with flour. Stack on a plate with a piece of oiled parchment between each oval. At this point, the plate of flatbreads can be tightly wrapped in foil and refrigerated about 2 hours.

4. When you are ready to cook, brush both sides of each oval lightly with olive oil. Dip your fingertips into water and press down into the dough to create small indentations. Sprinkle each oval with sesame seeds and/or rosemary.

5. Arrange the breads on the hot grate over medium-low coals and grill for about 4 minutes, until the side on the grill is golden and crusty. Flip the flatbreads and cook the other side for 4 minutes.

6. Transfer breads to a serving platter and serve warm.

NO-RISE GRILLED CHICAMA FLATBREADS

QUINOA SHRIMP SALAD

Serves 4

Quinoa is fast becoming the grain of choice among health food advocates, but it has been a staple in Peru and Ecuador for centuries, dating back to the ancient Incas, who lived high up in the Andes and used it mainly as a cereal. It has a wonderful nutty flavor and aroma that is intensified if you lightly toast the grains in a hot, dry skillet for a few minutes before cooking them in stock or water.

QUINOA

1 cup quinoa

2 cups water

1 tablespoon butter

1 teaspoon salt

$^1/_4$ cup fresh peas

$^1/_4$ cup cooked corn kernels

1 pound medium shrimp, peeled and deveined

3 tablespoons Barbecue Spice Rub (page 151)

2 tablespoons vegetable oil

$^1/_4$ cup finely diced red bell pepper

4 scallions, green part only, thinly sliced

2 tablespoons finely chopped parsley

2 tablespoons mayonnaise

Juice of 1 lemon

Salt and freshly ground black pepper

1. To prepare the quinoa, gently rinse the grains under cold running water. Combine the quinoa, water, butter, and salt in a saucepan and bring to a boil. Lower the heat to a simmer, cover, and continue to cook for 20 minutes, until the grain is tender and the water is absorbed. Transfer the cooked quinoa to a bowl.

2. Meanwhile, blanch the peas in boiling salted water for 3 to 4 minutes. Drain and plunge into ice water to stop the cooking. Cook the corn in boiling salted water for 3 to 4 minutes. Drain and plunge into ice water to stop the cooking. Drain both vegetables and set aside.

3. Prepare a hot fire in the grill. Set a vegetable/fish grill rack on the grill grate.

4. Toss the shrimp with the spice mixture and rub with oil. Arrange on the hot rack and grill for 1 to 2 minutes per side, until the shrimp have turned bright pink on the outside and white on the inside.

5. Transfer the cooked shrimp to a cutting board, chop into $^1/_2$-inch pieces, and fold into the quinoa. Add the peas, corn, bell pepper, scallions, parsley, mayonnaise, lemon juice, and salt and pepper.

6. Serve at once, or refrigerate and serve chilled.

SALAD SALAD SALAD SALAD SALAD SAL

SUMMER'S-ALMOST-GONE SWEET POTATO SALAD

Serves 8

Andrew and his mom, Mary Ellen, created this recipe at Andrew's house on the Jersey shore on one of the last days of summer. When we tested the salad at the restaurant, the staff rallied for changing the name to "We-NEVER-Want-Summer-to-End Potato Salad." The salad can be made ahead of time and refrigerated. But remember, all potato salads taste best at room temperature. So if you make it ahead of time and refrigerate it, remove the salad from the refrigerator 30 to 60 minutes to allow it to come to room temperature before serving.

1 pound sweet potatoes, peeled and
   cut into $^1/_2$-inch dice

1 pound boniatos, peeled and cut into $^1/_2$-inch dice

1 tablespoon butter

2 tablespoons vegetable oil

2 cups diced Spanish onion

Salt and freshly ground black pepper

$^1/_4$ cup chopped scallion, green parts only

$^1/_4$ cup finely chopped celery

2 tablespoons chopped pecans

2 tablespoons golden raisins

2 tablespoons dried cranberries

$^1/_2$ cup crème fraîche

2 tablespoons American-style yellow mustard

$1^1/_2$ teaspoons Tabasco sauce

3 tablespoons coarsely chopped fresh parsley

1. In a large pot, combine the sweet potatoes and boniatos with enough salted water to cover, bring to a boil, then lower heat to a simmer and gently cook for 10 to 15 minutes, being careful not to overcook. When the sweet potatoes are fork tender, drain and shake the pot over medium heat until all the moisture has evaporated. Transfer to a large bowl.

2. In a sauté pan over high heat, melt the butter with the vegetable oil. Add the diced onion and season with salt and pepper. Stir and continue to cook until the onions are caramelized, about 10 minutes. Add to the sweet potatoes. Gently fold in the scallion, celery, pecans, raisins, cranberries, crème fraîche, mustard, Tabasco, and parsley.

3. Serve at room temperature.

SALAD SALAD SALAD SALAD

MANCHEGO CORNMEAL BISCUITS

Makes 12

Bake these biscuits ahead of time (even the night before you entertain), and quickly grill them just before serving to give them that smoky flavor and faint char marks.

1 cup yellow cornmeal

1 cup all-purpose flour

1 tablespoon baking powder

1/2 teaspoon baking soda

1 teaspoon salt

1 teaspoon sugar

1/4 teaspoon cayenne pepper

2 teaspoons finely chopped rosemary leaves

6 tablespoons unsalted butter, melted and cooled

1 egg

3/4 to 1 cup buttermilk

1/3 cup coarsely chopped golden raisins

1 cup coarsely grated Manchego cheese

1. Preheat the oven to 350°F. Line a baking sheet with parchment paper and set aside.

2. In a medium bowl, combine the cornmeal, flour, baking powder and soda, salt, sugar, cayenne, and rosemary.

3. In a separate bowl, whisk together the butter, egg, and buttermilk.

4. Gradually add the buttermilk mixture to the dry ingredients, mixing just enough to combine and produce a crumbly dough. Fold in the raisins and cheese.

5. Scoop out 1/4-cup sized balls of dough with an ice cream scoop, pat intro rounds, and drop onto the prepared baking sheet.

6. Bake the biscuits for about 20 minutes, until the bottoms are golden brown. Transfer to a cooling rack and cool for 10 minutes.

7. To serve, reheat the biscuits on the grill until warm and faint grill marks appear on the tops and bottoms.

MANCHEGO CORNMEAL BISCUITS

GRILLED HEARTS OF PALM AND CHERRY TOMATO SALAD

Serves 8

Fresh hearts of palm should be firm, white, and free of any moisture or smell. Peel away any dark spots with an ordinary potato peeler to get to their natural snowy white color. Hearts of palm are imported from Brazil and Costa Rica. See Sources (page 183) to locate them.

1 lemon, halved

3 bay leaves

1 small onion, sliced

2 tablespoons salt

1 tablespoon whole black peppercorns

8 fresh hearts of palm

2 pints cherry tomatoes, yellow and red, cut in half

1 medium red onion, thinly sliced

2 tablespoons julienned fresh basil leaves

1 tablespoon coarsely chopped flat-leaf parsley

1 tablespoon chopped garlic

1 teaspoon crushed red pepper flakes

6 tablespoons olive oil

$1/4$ cup aged sherry wine vinegar

Salt and freshly ground black pepper

1. Prepare a medium fire in the grill.

2. In a large pot, bring 2 quarts of water to a boil with the lemon halves, bay leaves, onion, salt, and peppercorns. Add the fresh hearts of palm and blanch for 2 to 3 minutes. Drain, plunge into ice water to stop the cooking process, and drain again. Place the hearts of palm on a towel-lined plate.

3. Oil the grate. Arrange the hearts of palm on the hot grate and grill until grill marks appear on all sides, about 7 minutes. Remove from the grill and set aside on a plate to cool.

4. Meanwhile, prepare the tomato salad by mixing together the tomatoes, onion, basil, parsley, garlic, red pepper, oil, vinegar, and salt and pepper.

5. Slice the hearts of palm $1/8$ inch thick at a slight angle. Toss with the cherry tomato salad and serve.

GRILLED SALADS

GRILLED MUSHROOM SALSA

Serves 8

We usually invite twenty to thirty guests to most of our barbecue parties, and there are always a couple of vegetarians in the bunch. This mushroom salsa becomes a flavoring agent for most of the vegetarian dishes, and we seem to run out of it quickly every time. It's also a nice topping for any grilled meat.

VINAIGRETTE

1/4 cup fresh thyme leaves

2 tablespoons fresh marjoram leaves

1/4 cup coarsely chopped cilantro

3 cloves garlic, chopped fine

1/4 cup minced shallots

1/4 cup aged sherry wine vinegar

1/4 cup olive oil

Salt and freshly ground black pepper

8 ounces large shiitake mushroom caps

8 ounces medium-sized button mushrooms

2 large portobello mushrooms, stems removed and dark gills underneath scraped off

4 ounces dried black trumpet mushrooms

1 large white onion, cut in half crosswise

1/2 cup chopped scallions, green parts only

2 large roasted red bell peppers (page 179), cut into 1/4-inch dice

1/4 cup truffle oil

Salt and freshly ground black pepper

1. To make the vinaigrette, combine the thyme, marjoram, cilantro, garlic, and shallots in a food processor. Pulse to finely chop. Add the vinegar and pulse to combine. With the motor running, add the oil in a slow steady stream until emulsified. Season with salt and pepper.

2. Combine the shiitakes, button mushrooms, and portobellos in a large bowl. Add half the vinaigrette and toss to mix well. Set aside to marinate for at least 1 hour, but no more than 2 hours.

3. Meanwhile, prepare a medium-hot fire in the grill.

4. In a small bowl, cover the black trumpet mushrooms with boiling water and leave to soak for 10 minutes. Drain and discard the soaking water. Cover again with boiling water and leave to soak for 10 minutes. Drain and discard the soaking water. Chop the mushrooms into fine pieces.

5. Place the onion on the hot grate and grill until tender, turning frequently, about 15 minutes. Cut into 1/4-inch dice.

6. Place a vegetable/fish grill rack on the grate. Place the marinated mushrooms on the hot rack and grill for about 2 minutes on each side, being careful not to burn them. Transfer to a bowl. When cool, dice the mushrooms into 1/2-inch pieces and return to the bowl. Add the black trumpet mushrooms, onion, scallions, roasted peppers, truffle oil, and the remaining half of the herb vinaigrette.

7. Season with salt and pepper, toss well, and serve at room temperature.

DESSERTS

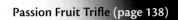

Passion Fruit Trifle (page 138)

BLACK QUINOA AND CLOVES CAKE

Serves 10

Hortensia, my assistant, was pastry chef at the Ballroom, owned by Chef Felipe Rojas Lombardi, who was a role model for me even though I never had the opportunity to meet him. Felipe developed a quinoa-based cake, which Hortensia tested and baked for him. It was garnished with a European custard buttercream and became a staple at the restaurant. Since we use black quinoa at my restaurant, Hortensia revamped the cake and came up with the following version. If you can't find black quinoa, the regular grain will work fine.

1 tablespoon unsalted butter, to grease pan

3 tablespoons ground walnuts, to dust pan

1 1/3 cups black quinoa, unrinsed

6 cups water

1/2 cup unsalted butter (4 ounces),
  at room temperature

3/4 cup light brown sugar, firmly packed

2 teaspoons ground cloves

1 teaspoon ground cinnamon

1/2 teaspoon salt

5 eggs plus 1 egg yolk

1/4 cup all-purpose flour

1/2 cup finely chopped walnuts

3/4 cup heavy cream

1/4 cup dark rum

Zest of 1 lemon, minced

Confectioners' sugar or cream cheese frosting
  (page 132)

1. Preheat the oven to 325°F. Thoroughly butter an 8-inch springform pan or round cake pan. Pour the ground walnuts into the pan and swirl it so the whole inside of the pan is covered with nuts. Turn the pan upside down to remove any excess nuts.

2. In a sauté pan over medium heat, toast the quinoa for 1 minute while stirring continuously. The grains will crackle and give off a toasty smell. Reduce the heat to medium-low, keep stirring, and toast for another 4 minutes. Cool the quinoa to room temperature.

3. Combine the cooled quinoa with the water in a saucepan. Bring to a boil, reduce the heat, and simmer uncovered for about 10 minutes. The quinoa should taste nutty and be barely tender, not mushy. Strain in a fine strainer and set aside.

4. In the bowl of an electric mixer, combine the butter, sugar, cloves, cinnamon, and salt. Using the paddle attachment, cream the mixture on medium speed, adding the eggs and yolk one by one. Beating on low speed, add the flour, walnuts, heavy cream, rum, and lemon zest until just combined. Fold in the drained quinoa and combine well. Pour the cake batter into the prepared pan.

5. Bake for about 1 hour and 20 minutes, until a skewer inserted in the middle of the pan comes out clean.

6. Remove the cake from the oven and allow to cool in the pan for 30 minutes at room temperature. Remove the sides of the springform pan and allow the cake to cool for an additional 60 minutes. (Since the cake batter has no gluten except for the flour, and only the eggs and yolk act as binder, the cake is very moist and will collapse if removed from the pan while still warm.) Invert it onto a plate, then turn it right side up onto a serving plate.

7. Dust with confectioners' sugar or frost the top and sides with cream cheese frosting.

8. Slice and serve.

HORTENSIA'S BEST-EVER CHOCOLATE POUND CAKE

Serves 12

"Got milk?" You'll need it for this slice of chocolate heaven. Everyone who has ever tried this chocolate cake has said it was the best they've had. Some want a second and even a third slice. It's my assistant Hortensia's recipe. She's the most exact baker I have ever met, constantly trying to perfect what is already perfect. (In fact she recommends the specific brand of cocoa called for below, which is available from King Arthur Flour; other brands will work, but the texture of the cake will not be the same.)

Unsalted butter, at room temperature (but still firm), to brush pan

$^1/_4$ cup sugar, to line pan

2 cups all-purpose flour

1 cup plus 2 tablespoons unsweetened Van Leer Dutch process medium cocoa

1 teaspoon baking powder

$^1/_2$ teaspoon baking soda

1 teaspoon salt

$1^1/_2$ cups unsalted butter, at room temperature

$2^3/_4$ cups sugar

2 teaspoons vanilla extract

2 teaspoons espresso extract
    (or substitute 2 teaspoons instant coffee dissolved in 1 tablespoon buttermilk)

5 eggs

$1^1/_4$ cups buttermilk

Cocoa powder or confectioners' sugar, to finish

1. Preheat the oven to 325°F. Brush a 10-inch Bundt pan with the room-temperature (but still firm) unsalted butter. Pour $^1/_4$ cup sugar into the pan, swirling the sugar in the pan so that the chimney and sides are covered well. Turn the pan upside down to remove any excess sugar and set aside.

2. Sift together the flour, cocoa, baking powder, baking soda, and salt.

3. Into the bowl of an electric mixer fitted with a paddle, cream the butter on medium speed. Add the sugar and beat until the mixture is light and fluffy. Scrape down the bowl with a rubber spatula. Beating at medium speed, add the vanilla, espresso extract, and the eggs, one by one, beating only until they are well blended.

4. Beating on low speed, add a third of the flour mixture and a third of the buttermilk. Do this twice more with the remaining dry ingredients and buttermilk, scraping the bowl with a rubber spatula in between. Finally, beat the batter on medium speed for 30 seconds, until it is smooth.

5. Pour the batter into the prepared pan. Bake the cake for 50 to 60 minutes, until the top feels springy and a toothpick inserted in the middle comes out clean.

6. Cool the cake in the pan on a wire rack for about 20 minutes. Then turn it out onto the wire rack to finish cooling.

7. To finish, dust the cake with cocoa or confectioners' sugar.

CHERRY-ALMOND POUND CAKE

Serves 12

This cake has become a Thanksgiving tradition at my house. My wife, Trish, always has Hortensia make one, and I like to serve it with ice cream. At Thanksgiving, "Horty" makes it with a combination of dried and fresh cranberries, a variation she created especially for me when I was invited to the World Gourmet Summit in Singapore.

$1/4$ cup amaretto liqueur

1 cup coarsely chopped dried cherries

3 cups all-purpose flour

1 teaspoon baking powder

$1/2$ teaspoon baking soda

$1/2$ teaspoon salt

4 ounces almond paste, at room temperature

$2^1/2$ cups sugar

$1^1/4$ cups unsalted butter

6 eggs

$1/2$ teaspoon bitter almond extract
  (or substitute almond extract)

1 cup sour cream

GLAZE

2 tablespoons amaretto liqueur

$1^1/2$ cups confectioners' sugar

1. About 2 hours before you are ready to bake, heat the amaretto in a small saucepan. Add the dried cherries. Let cool, stirring occasionally, until the cherries have soaked up all the liquid.

2. Preheat the oven to 325°F. Butter and flour a 10-inch Bundt pan, tapping out any excess flour.

3. Sift together the flour, baking powder, baking soda, and salt. Set aside.

4. In a large mixing bowl fitted with a paddle, combine the almond paste and sugar. Beat on low speed until well combined and the mixture looks like wet sand. Add the butter and beat at medium speed until very fluffy, about 3 minutes. Scrape down the bowl with a rubber spatula and add the almond extract and the eggs, one by one, beating only until they are well blended.

5. Beating on low speed, add a third of the dry ingredients and a third of the sour cream. Do this twice more with the remaining dry ingredients and sour cream, scraping the bowl with a rubber spatula. Finally, beat the batter for about 20 seconds, until it is smooth looking. By hand, fold in the cherries until they are well distributed in the batter.

6. Pour the batter into the prepared pan. Level the top with a spatula and tap the pan gently on the counter to settle the batter evenly.

7. Bake for 50 to 60 minutes, until the top is browned and feels springy, and a toothpick inserted in the middle comes out clean.

8. Allow the cake to cool in the pan for 20 minutes, then turn it out onto a wire rack to finish cooling.

9. Make the glaze while the cake is cooling. Sift the confectioners' sugar into a small bowl and slowly blend in the amaretto with a fork until the mixture is smooth.

10. Drizzle the cake with the glaze while the cake is still warm.

FIESTA ANGEL CAKE

Serves 12

When my wife, Trish, asked Hortensia to make a fat-free cake, this is the one Horty created. I like it best with just the grated lime zest and dried whole cranberries. The technique of using hot liquid in the batter gives the cake more body, making it the perfect base for a trifle or any fruit dessert. Leftovers should be wrapped well in plastic wrap and can be frozen.

1^1/$_2$ cups all-purpose flour

1^3/$_4$ cups sugar

^{1}/$_4$ cup cornstarch

2^1/$_2$ teaspoons baking powder

^{1}/$_2$ teaspoon salt

1 cup boiling water or fruit juice

Zest of 1 lime or lemon, minced

2 teaspoons lemon extract

1^1/$_3$ cups egg whites (about 9 egg whites)

1 teaspoon cream of tartar

^{1}/$_3$ cup dried fruit (combination of pineapple, mango, cherries, or cranberries)

1. Sift the flour, 1^1/$_4$ cups of the sugar, the cornstarch, baking powder, and salt into the bowl of an electric mixer. On very low speed, using the paddle attachment, combine the mixture for 30 seconds.

2. In a small saucepan, bring the water to a boil. While the mixer is running on low speed, pour the boiling water over the dry ingredients. Increase the speed to medium-low and continue beating. The batter will first look very doughy; after about 2 minutes, it will start to look almost transparent and glossy. Scrape the bowl with a spatula and beat for 1 more minute.

3. Let the flour mixture cool to room temperature. Gently fold in the zest and lemon extract.

4. Preheat the oven to 325°F.

5. Pour the egg whites into a clean mixing bowl. Fill a medium-size saucepan with water and bring to a boil. Turn off the heat and place the mixing bowl over, but not touching, the hot water. Beat the whites by hand with a whisk until the mixture is frothy and the whites feel very warm to the touch. Attach the bowl to the electric mixer, add the cream of tartar, and beat the whites on medium-high speed, just until they hold soft peaks. Pour in the remaining ^{1}/$_2$ cup sugar and continue to beat until the mixture forms firm peaks.

6. With a spatula, fold one-quarter of the beaten whites into the cooled flour mixture until thoroughly combined. Pour this lightened flour mixture over the remaining egg whites and add the dried fruit. Fold together gently, but thoroughly.

7. Pour the batter into an ungreased 10-inch tube pan with removable bottom and place on a baking sheet.

8. Bake on a rack in the middle of the oven for 45 minutes, until the top is springy and golden brown.

9. Remove the pan from the oven and immediately invert it over the neck of a bottle. Do not disturb until the cake is completely cool, about 1 hour.

10. Gently loosen the sides of the cake by running a knife blade snugly around the sides. Transfer the cake to a serving plate.

11. Slice with a serrated knife and serve.

BLACK LEMON–POPPY SEED CAKE

Serves 12

This cake was inspired by Chef Felipe Rojas Lombardi, who once mentioned to Hortensia that he had developed a very striking black cake, with the outside covered by poppy seeds. So she created her own version and repeated the black streak inside. Sliced and grilled, then served with berries or just plain, this cake makes a wonderful barbecue party dessert.

Unsalted butter, at room temperature (but still firm), to brush pan

$1/2$ cup poppy seeds, to line pan

3 cups plus 2 tablespoons all-purpose flour

$1/2$ teaspoon salt

$1/2$ teaspoon baking soda

$1 1/2$ cups unsalted butter

$2 1/2$ cups sugar

2 teaspoons lemon extract

6 eggs

1 cup sour cream

Zest of 3 lemons

$1/3$ cup poppy seeds

GLAZE

$1/2$ cup freshly squeezed lemon juice

$3/4$ cup sugar

1. Preheat the oven to 325°F. Thoroughly butter a 10-inch Bundt pan with a brush, making sure that the whole pan, including the chimney, is covered. It should have an opaque film so that the seeds will cover the whole inside. Pour $1/2$ cup of the poppy seeds into the pan and swirl it so that the whole pan is covered with the seeds. Turn the pan upside down to remove any excess seeds.

2. Sift together the flour, salt, and baking soda. Set aside.

3. In a large mixing bowl fitted with a paddle attachment, beat the butter on medium speed until very fluffy, about 3 minutes. Add the sugar and continue beating until the mixture is light and fluffy. Scrape down the bowl with a rubber spatula, add the lemon extract and the eggs, one by one, beating only until they are well blended.

4. On low speed, add a third of the dry ingredients and a third of the sour cream. Do this twice more with the remaining dry ingredients and sour cream, scraping the bowl with a rubber spatula. Finally, beat the batter for about 1 minute, until it is smooth looking. By hand stir in the lemon zest and combine well.

5. Remove 1 cup of the batter and combine with the $1/3$ cup poppy seeds. Set aside.

6. Pour half of the remaining plain batter into the prepared pan. With the back of a teaspoon, make a $1/2$-inch-deep trench halfway between the chimney and the outside of the pan. Carefully distribute the poppy seed batter in the trench and cover with the remaining plain batter. Level the top with a spatula and tap the pan gently on the counter to settle the batter evenly.

7. Bake for 50 to 60 minutes, until the top is browned and feels springy, and a toothpick inserted in the middle comes out clean.

8. Allow the cake to cool in the pan for about 20 minutes, then turn it out onto a wire rack to finish cooling.

9. Prepare the glaze while the cake is cooling. In a small saucepan, combine the lemon juice and sugar and bring to a boil, stirring until the sugar is dissolved. Lower the heat and simmer for 3 minutes.

10. While it is still warm, brush the cake all over with 1 cup of the hot lemon glaze, always waiting until the cake has absorbed the glaze before brushing on more.

GINGER-SPICED CARROT CAKE WITH CREAM CHEESE FROSTING

Serves 12

Our friends, Don and Christine Pintabona, love carrot cake, so one day, when we knew they were coming over, I had Hortensia bake them one. As usual, Don stopped by his Italian Brooklyn Bakery to pick up cookies, cheesecake, and other goodies, so we had plenty of sweet things on hand. I ended up eating most of the cake myself…in two days! Horty insists on including the weight for the grated carrots because cups are less precise and slightly more or less than 17 ounces will affect the texture of the cake.

CAKE

2¹/₂ cups all-purpose flour

2¹/₂ teaspoons baking powder

1¹/₄ teaspoons baking soda

2 teaspoons ground cinnamon

1 teaspoon ground allspice

1 teaspoon ground ginger

¹/₂ teaspoon salt

4 eggs

³/₄ cup granulated sugar

1 cup light brown sugar

2 tablespoons honey

1¹/₄ cups canola oil

Juice of 1 orange

Zest of 1 orange, minced

3 cups packed peeled, grated carrots (about 5 to 6 whole, 17 ounces grated)

6 pieces (1¹/₂ ounces) Australian or other candied ginger, cut into thin slivers

1 cup walnut pieces

1 cup golden raisins

CREAM CHEESE FROSTING

8 ounces cream cheese, softened

3 cups confectioners' sugar

Zest of 1 orange, minced

1. Preheat the oven to 325°F. Butter and flour a 10-inch Bundt pan, inverting the pan and tapping out any excess flour. Set aside.

2. Sift together the flour, baking powder, baking soda, cinnamon, allspice, ground ginger, and salt.

3. In a large mixing bowl fitted with a paddle, combine the eggs, granulated sugar, and brown sugar. Blend on medium speed until light and fluffy. On low speed, add the honey and a third of the dry ingredients. Still beating, alternate adding the oil and orange juice with the remaining dry ingredients.

4. Fold in the orange zest, grated carrots, candied ginger, walnuts, and raisins until evenly distributed.

5. Pour the batter into the prepared pan and bake for about 1 hour, or until a cake tester inserted in the middle of the cake comes out clean.

6. Cool the cake in the pan on a wire rack for 20 minutes. Then turn it out onto the wire rack to finish cooling.

7. While the cake is cooling, prepare the frosting. In a small bowl, beat together the cream cheese and sugar with a hand mixer until smooth. Fold in the zest.

8. Frost the cooled cake.

LATIN SPICE COOKIES

Makes 80

Last Christmas, Hortensia made these cookies for my family—we love them almost as much as we love her! She uses a generous amount of dry unsweetened coconut for extra crispness and sliced almonds for texture. If you don't want to bake the dough immediately, wrap the chilled cylinders in plastic wrap and freeze. When you are ready to bake, cut frozen dough into $1/8$-inch-thick slices, arrange on a parchment paper–lined baking sheet, and bake as directed. The spice mix recipe makes more than you'll need, but you can use the leftover mix to flavor the crust for a pumpkin cheesecake or the topping of a fruit crisp.

GROUND SPICE MIX

$1/4$ teaspoon plus $1/8$ teaspoon white pepper

$1^1/2$ teaspoons ground cardamom

1 tablespoon ground ginger

1 tablespoon plus $3/4$ teaspoon ground cloves

1 tablespoon plus $3/4$ teaspoon ground nutmeg

$1/4$ cup plus $1^1/2$ teaspoons ground cinnamon

DOUGH

8 ounces unsalted butter, at room temperature

$3/4$ cup sugar

$1/2$ cup blanched sliced almonds

1 cup unsweetened coconut

$1^1/2$ cups all-purpose flour

1. Combine all the spices in a small jar with a lid and set aside.

2. In an electric mixer fitted with a paddle, cream the butter and sugar on medium speed. While beating on low speed, add 2 tablespoons of the spice mix and the sliced almonds and beat until the nuts have broken up into small pieces. Slowly add the coconut and $1^1/2$ cups of the flour. Add more flour as needed; the dough should be sticky, but not dry.

3. On a lightly floured work surface, pat the dough into a large rectangle. Cut the rectangle into 2 equal pieces. Roll each piece into an 11-inch-long cylinder about $1^3/4$ inches in diameter. Wrap the cylinders in parchment paper and refrigerate for at least 1 hour.

4. Preheat the oven to 350°F. Line a baking sheet with parchment paper.

5. On a lightly floured surface, slice the rolls into $1/4$-inch-wide rounds. Arrange the cookies 1 inch apart on the baking sheet.

6. Bake for 12 to 15 minutes, until the cookies are set and the edges are lightly browned. Let cool on the baking sheet for 5 minutes, then transfer to a cooling rack to complete cooling.

MANTECADITOS

Makes about 55 cookies

Hortensia's dear friend, Cusy Miranda, who was born in Puerto Rico, introduced her to these tender white almond cookies, and she fell in love with them. The name translates as "little pork fat cookies," but we substitute vegetable shortening for the lard. We add sliced almonds, which give the Mantecaditos great texture, since you get different-size nut pieces in the dough.

1/2 cup unsalted butter, at room temperature

1/2 cup solid vegetable shortening

3/4 cup superfine sugar

1/2 cup sliced blanched almonds

1 teaspoon bitter almond extract or almond extract

1/2 teaspoon salt

2 to 2 1/4 cups all-purpose flour

Confectioners' sugar

1. Preheat the oven to 325°F. Line 2 cookie sheets with parchment paper.

2. In an electric mixer, combine the butter, shortening, and sugar. Using the paddle attachment on medium speed, cream the mixture. With the mixer on low speed, add the almonds and process for 1 minute, until the nuts have broken up. With the mixer still running on low, add the extract, salt, and 1 1/2 cups flour. Continue to add flour, 2 tablespoons at a time, until the dough is smooth and just holds together, but does not crumble.

3. Shape the dough into balls with a 1 1/4-inch ice cream scoop and arrange on the cookie sheet.

4. Bake for 12 to 15 minutes. The cookies will be pale but the bottoms will be golden brown. Roll the warm cookies in confectioners' sugar.

5. Cool the cookies to room temperature and serve, or place them in a plastic bag, seal, and store in a metal tin.

MANTECADITOS

MANGO RICE CAKES

Makes 12

These tender, extra-large rice cookie-like cakes go nicely with the Chilled Watermelon–Peach Soup (page 140) or to nibble on anytime you're craving a sweet that's not too sweet. These cookie-cakes are best the same day they're baked or the day after.

CAKES

1/2 cup unsalted butter, at room temperature

1 cup sugar

1 egg

3 tablespoons sour cream

2 cups all-purpose flour

1 1/2 teaspoons baking powder

1 teaspoon vanilla extract

1/2 teaspoon salt

3/4 cup cooked short-grain rice

1 tablespoon finely minced candied ginger

1/3 cup chopped dried mango pieces

SPICE COATING

1/4 cup granulated sugar

1/2 teaspoon ground cardamom

1. Preheat the oven to 350°F. Line a baking sheet with parchment paper.

2. In a mixing bowl fitted with a paddle attachment, cream the butter with the sugar on medium speed. Add the egg and beat to combine. Beating on low speed, add the sour cream, flour, baking powder, vanilla, salt, rice, candied ginger, and dried mango.

3. Transfer the dough to a lightly floured surface and, with floured hands, shape it into a rectangle 1/4 inch thick. Cut out cookies with a 3-inch-diameter cookie cutter. Arrange on the baking sheet.

4. Combine the sugar and cardamom. Sprinkle the spice mixture over the cakes.

5. Bake for 13 to 15 minutes or until golden brown. Transfer to a cooling rack to cool.

RICE CAKES

MANGO

DOUBLE CHOCOLATE—COCONUT S'MORES

Makes 12

Sam De Marco serves these at First Restaurant, but you can make your own. This recipe is great for kids. Unlike traditional marshmallows made from scratch, these are a breeze because the sugar does not have to be boiled and fussed over.

MARSHMALLOWS

1 tablespoon plus 1 teaspoon unflavored gelatin

1/3 cup cold water

1/2 cup granulated sugar

2/3 cup light corn syrup

1/2 teaspoon vanilla extract

1/2 cup confectioners' sugar

1/2 cup cornstarch

2 cups plus 2/3 cup flaked coconut, toasted

**22 chocolate graham crackers
(12 whole crackers, broken in half)**

1 pound semisweet chocolate, melted

1. To make the marshmallows, combine the gelatin and cold water in a small metal bowl and stir well to dissolve. Let the mixture sit until it becomes firm.

2. In a small saucepan, bring about 2 cups of water to a boil. Remove from the heat and nest the bowl of gelatin mixture in it until the gelatin has liquified and is very warm. Add the sugar and stir well to dissolve.

3. Pour the mixture into a mixing bowl and add the corn syrup and vanilla. Beat on medium-high speed with the whisk attachment for 10 to 12 minutes, until the marshmallow mixture is very thick and fluffy.

4. Combine the confectioners' sugar and cornstarch in a small bowl. Lightly butter an 8-inch square pan and liberally sprinkle with some of the combined sugar and cornstarch, reserving some of the mixture. Pour the marshmallow mixture into the pan, smooth the top, and refrigerate at least overnight.

5. Remove from the refrigerator and sprinkle the top surface with more of the sugar-cornstarch mixture. Loosen the sides of the pan with a spatula and remove the marshmallow mixture from the pan in one piece, turning it out onto a baking sheet dusted with more of the sugar-cornstarch mixture. The marshmallow will be sticky until thoroughly coated with the sugar-cornstarch mixture.

6. Dip scissors in cold water and cut the marshmallow into 2-inch squares. Roll each square in the sugar-cornstarch coating mixture and place on a rack to dry for several hours. In an airtight container, they will stay moist for about 3 weeks.

7. To make the s'mores, preheat the oven to 275°F. Distribute the coconut evenly on a baking sheet and toast in the oven for 15 to 20 minutes, or until golden.

8. Line a baking sheet with aluminum foil. Place the crackers top side down on the foil, generously slather them with the melted chocolate, and sprinkle with toasted coconut. Place 1 marshmallow over the coconut and top with another cracker, bottom side down.

9. When the coals in the grill are reduced to a slow, glowing ash, transfer the baking sheet to the grill, cover the grill, and roast for 4 to 5 minutes, until the marshmallows have melted. Serve warm.

PASSION FRUIT TRIFLE

Serves 10 to 12

Every Thanksgiving, I cater a feast for The Late Show with David Letterman. *Last year Hortensia added a new item to the dessert selection—a trifle. The staff loved it and so did our crew.*

SYRUP

1 cup passion fruit purée

1 cup sugar

CUSTARD

2 tablespoons plus 2 teaspoons cornstarch

¹/₄ teaspoon salt

5 egg yolks

2¹/₂ cups milk

6 tablespoons sugar

2 teaspoons vanilla extract

1 Fiesta Angel Cake (page 129), cut into cubes or 2-inch slices

3 ripe mangoes, peeled and cubed

GARNISH

1 cup whipping cream, chilled

¹/₄ cup confectioners' sugar

1 tablespoon dark rum

1 pint fresh raspberries (optional)

1 pint fresh blueberries (optional)

1. To make the syrup, simmer the passion fruit purée and sugar in a small saucepan, stirring until the sugar is dissolved, about 5 minutes. Set aside.

2. To make the custard, combine the cornstarch, salt, and yolks in a small bowl and whisk to blend.

3. In a heavy, medium saucepan, combine the milk and sugar and bring to a boil. Take the saucepan off the heat and whisk 1 cup of the hot milk into the yolk mixture. Strain the yolk mixture back into the saucepan and cook over medium heat, stirring continuously, until the custard thickens and comes to a boil. Cook for 1 minute and blend in the vanilla. Transfer to a bowl, place a piece of plastic wrap directly on the custard, and refrigerate.

4. To assemble the trifle, spoon a thin layer of the custard over the bottom of a 3- to 4-quart trifle bowl. Make sure it goes right to the edge so that the custard shows. Top with a layer of cake cubes or slices, drizzle with some syrup and cover the cake cubes with a layer of custard. Spoon about ¹/₂ cup of the mangoes over the custard and top with more cake pieces and syrup. Again, add more custard, mangoes, and cake and finish with a layer of fruit. Cover the bowl with plastic and chill for up to 1 day.

5. When you are ready to serve, beat the chilled cream with the confectioners' sugar and rum until soft peaks are formed. Garnish the trifle with the whipped cream and berries, if using, and serve.

CHILLED WATERMELON-PEACH SOUP

Serves 4 to 6

I had a watermelon sorbet made with rioja wine on the menu and we all liked it so much that Hortensia got the idea to make a soup using it as a base. She added velvety peach juice to smooth out the consistency.

1/2 cup champagne vinegar

1/4 cup honey

1 tablespoon coarsely chopped plus 1 tablespoon julienned Huacatay leaves (substitute fresh mint leaves)

1 1/2 pounds fresh watermelon

1 1/2 pounds fresh peaches

1/4 cup sugar

1. Combine the vinegar and honey in a small saucepan, bring to a boil, and immediately lower to a simmer. Add the chopped huacatay leaves and cook on low until the liquid is reduced by half and thick and syrupy. Set aside.

2. Cut the watermelon away from the rind and remove the seeds. Set aside.

3. Peel the peaches, cut in half, and remove the pits. Place the peaches in a medium saucepan. Add the sugar and remaining chopped huacatay, and cook over medium-low heat until the peaches are tender, about 10 minutes. Set aside to cool to room temperature.

4. In the pitcher of an electric blender, purée the peaches. Add the watermelon and champagne vinegar reduction, and pass it through a fine strainer. Refrigerate until serving time.

5. Ladle the soup into martini glasses or shallow soup bowls. Garnish with the julienned huacatay and serve.

CHILLED WATERMELON-PEACH SOUP

COOL SPICED FLAN

Serves 12

How can you tell when a flan is done? Hortensia's mentor, chef Felipe Rojas Lombardi, always said, "The middle shakes like a lady's belly." This is another recipe Horty prepared for me to take to the World Gourmet Summit in Singapore. The caramel with the annatto seeds gives the flan a magnificent orange hue.

If you want to make fewer flans than 12, you may use the extra custard base to make a rich ice cream. Just fill the desired number of ramekins, then pour the remaining flan mixture into a small saucepan and bring it to a simmer, never letting it boil. Continue to simmer slowly until thickened enough to leave a "track" in the custard on the back of a wooden spoon when you drag your fingertip through it. Remove the custard from the heat and set aside to cool completely. Freeze the cooled mixture in an ice cream maker and serve with the flan.

FLAN

1 1/2 cups heavy cream

1/2 cup milk

1/2 cup sugar

1 small cinnamon stick

1/2 vanilla bean, seeds included

3 whole eggs

2 yolks

CARAMEL

3/4 cup sugar

2 1/2 teaspoons annatto seeds

1/4 cup water

CARAMELIZED SPICES

3/4 cup sugar

1/4 cup water

About 10 small bay leaves, fresh or dry

About 10 star anise

1. To make the flan, combine the cream, milk, sugar, cinnamon, and vanilla in a saucepan and bring to a boil. Let cool for 15 minutes. Combine the eggs and yolks in a bowl and lightly break them up with a whisk. Slowly temper, stirring about 1/4 of the hot liquid into the eggs, and then incorporate the rest.

2. Preheat the oven to 350°F.

3. To make the caramel, combine the sugar, annatto seeds, and water in a heavy-bottomed saucepan over medium-low heat. Stir until the sugar dissolves and cook for about 15 minutes, until the sugar is a medium amber color. Remove from the heat, remove the annatto seeds with a small strainer, and pour the caramel into individual 4-ounce ramekins or molds.

4. Pour the flan mixture into the ramekins or molds, up to about 1/2 inch from the top. Place the ramekins in a baking dish and fill the dish with enough water to reach halfway up the sides of the flan molds. Cover the pan with aluminum foil.

5. Bake for 25 to 30 minutes, or until a paring knife inserted a third of the way toward the middle of a test flan mold comes out clean. Remove from the oven and let cool completely.

6. While the flan is cooling, make the caramelized spices. Combine the sugar and water in a heavy-bottomed saucepan over medium-low heat. Stir until the sugar dissolves and cook for about 15 minutes, until the sugar is a medium amber color. Remove from the heat and add the bay leaves and star anise to coat with the caramel. Let cool, remove the individual spices, let any excess caramel drip off, and place on parchment paper.

7. When you are ready to serve, run a knife around the inside edges of the individual ramekins or molds and invert the flans onto individual plates. Place 1 bay leaf and star anise on top of each individual flan.

VANILLA CUSTARD
WITH STRAWBERRIES AND LATIN SPICE COOKIES

Serves 6

A simple but very tasty and refreshing dessert that can be assembled ahead of time like a trifle in a glass bowl or, more elegantly, in a "rocks" or martini glass.

VANILLA CUSTARD

2 tablespoons plus 2 teaspoons cornstarch

¹/₄ teaspoon salt

5 egg yolks

2¹/₂ cups milk

6 tablespoons sugar

1 teaspoon vanilla extract

1 pound fresh strawberries

18 Latin Spice Cookies (page 133)

1. To make the custard, combine the cornstarch, salt, and yolks in a small bowl. Whisk to blend.

2. In a heavy medium-size saucepan, combine the milk and sugar and bring to a boil. Remove the saucepan from the heat and whisk 1 cup of the hot milk into the yolk mixture. Strain the yolk mixture back into the hot milk and place the saucepan over medium heat, until the custard thickens and comes to a boil. Cook for 1 minute, stirring continuously.

3. Transfer to a bowl, blend in the vanilla extract, place a piece of plastic wrap directly on the custard, and refrigerate.

4. Wash the strawberries under cold running water and place on a paper towel to dry. Stem and cut the strawberries in half (or quarters, if extra-large).

5. To assemble, place a layer of custard in each glass, followed by some strawberries and 2 spice cookies broken into quarters. Repeat with the remaining custard and strawberries, topping with 1 whole cookie. Serve chilled.

VANILLA CUSTARD WITH STRAWBERRIES

ESPRESSO CREAM

Serves 4

This simple and refreshing dessert can be made as much as a day ahead of time. Of course, you can make it a totally guilt-free dessert by replacing the whipped cream with a vanilla yogurt topping.

2 teaspoons gelatin

2 tablespoons water

1³/4 cups brewed coffee

2 tablespoons sugar

¹/4 cup Kahlúa

GARNISH

1 cup heavy cream

1 tablespoon confectioners' sugar

¹/4 teaspoon ground cinnamon

Chocolate-covered coffee beans (optional)

1. In a small metal bowl, moisten the gelatin with the water. Bring the coffee to a simmer in a small saucepan and add the sugar. Combine thoroughly with the gelatin mixture and stir in the coffee liqueur. Cover the bowl with plastic wrap and refrigerate for about 1 hour or until firm, stirring it with a fork every 20 minutes to give the finished gelatin an airy, bubbly texture.

2. Combine the heavy cream, sugar, and cinnamon in a small bowl and, with a hand mixer, whip it to very soft peaks.

3. Fill martini glasses three-quarters full with the coffee gelatin and top with the softly whipped cream. Garnish with the chocolate coffee beans, if you wish, and serve.

ESPRESSO

CREAM

SPICED PLUM CRISP

Serves 8

The first time we made this crisp in the restaurant, it never made it to the dining room because the kitchen staff devoured it. Since we had bought up all the fresh purple plums from the open market near us for the first crisp, Hortensia had to wait a whole week before she made more. It was a long week!

2 pounds fresh purple plums, pitted and halved

2 tablespoons sugar

1/4 teaspoon ground cloves

1/2 teaspoon ground nutmeg

1/2 teaspoon ground cinnamon

1 tablespoon all-purpose flour

1/3 cup port wine

TOPPING

1 2/3 cups all-purpose flour

1/4 teaspoon salt

1/4 teaspoon baking powder

2/3 cup sugar

1/2 teaspoon ground cardamom

9 tablespoons cold unsalted butter

1 quart vanilla ice cream

1. Preheat the oven to 350°F. Butter a 9 x 12-inch baking pan.

2. Toss the plums in a medium-size bowl with the sugar, spices, flour, and port. Layer the plum halves, cut side up, in the prepared pan.

3. To make the topping, mix the flour, salt, baking powder, sugar, and cardamom in a bowl. Cut the cold butter into small cubes and, with your hands, blend it with the dry mixture until it is crumbly. Sprinkle the topping over the plums and bake for 30 to 40 minutes, or until the plums are bubbling and the crumbs are golden brown.

4. Spoon into shallow serving bowls, and serve warm or at room temperature with vanilla ice cream on the side.

GRILL BASICS

OILS & RUBS

ANNATTO OIL ~ 150

ANISE-VANILLA OIL ~ 150

LEMON OIL ~ 150

RED CHILE OIL ~ 150

GARLIC OIL ~ 151

MOLE RUB ~ 151

BARBECUE SPICE RUB ~ 151

ADOBOS, GLAZES, & VINAIGRETTES

FISH ADOBO ~ 152

ORANGE-CORIANDER ADOBO ~ 152

ALIÑO ADOBO CRIOLLO ~ 153

DRIED MUSHROOM ADOBO ~ 153

GARLIC-LEMON-BEER ADOBO ~ 154

CHIPOTLE–RED WINE ADOBO ~ 155

ROSEMARY-HONEY-MUSTARD ADOBO ~ 155

PANELA RUM ADOBO ~ 155

JUNIPER BERRY–BAY LEAF RUM MARINADE ~ 156

RAIN FOREST GLAZE ~ 156

COSTA RICAN COFFEE GLAZE ~ 157

TAMARIND-RUM-SOY GLAZE ~ 157

RED PEPPER VINAIGRETTE ~ 158

GINGER VINAIGRETTE ~ 158

Ajis

GRILLED PINEAPPLE AJI ~ 159

OPAL BASIL CHIMICHURRI ~ 160

HUACATAY AJI ~ 161

PEBRE ~ 161

POBLANO–SERRANO CHILE AJI ~ 162

CALABAZA AJI ~ 162

HUEVO AJI ~ 163

MANI AJI ~ 163

CULANTRO AJI ~ 164

ROCOTO AJI ~ 164

SMOKED CHILE AJI ~ 166

HABANERO SATANICO AJI ~ 166

FAROFA DE MALAGUETA AJI ~ 167

Salsas, mojos, & miscellanea

OVEN-DRIED TOMATO AND FENNEL SALSA ~ 168

SUNCHOKE SALSA ~ 169

BANANA-LIME SALSA ~ 169

SMOKY CORN SALSA ~ 170

SEVEN LILY SALSA ~ 170

MANGO-MUSTARD SALSA ~ 171

BACALAO-CAPER SALSA ~ 171

SHALLOT-TRUFFLE MOJO ~ 172

MINT MOJO ~ 172

PASSION FRUIT MOJO ~ 173

STAR FRUIT MOJO ~ 173

TOMATILLO-POBLANO MARMALADE ~ 174

HABANERO SAUCE ~ 174

SAFFRON–AJI AMARILLO SAUCE ~ 175

TAMARIND TARTAR SAUCE ~ 175

LOBSTER STOCK ~ 176

SIMPLE SYRUP ~ 176

CHIPOTLE KETCHUP ~ 176

PICKLED JALAPEÑOS ~ 177

SWEET CORN–SAFFRON SAUCE ~ 177

OILS & RUBS

ANNATTO OIL

Makes about 1¹/₂ cups

Annato seeds are used in American cheddar to give it a rich orange-yellow color. The seeds also have an earthy flavor that complements many savory ingredients.

1 cup vegetable oil
¹/₂ cup annatto seeds

1. Heat the oil and seeds in a saucepan over low heat just until the oil begins to bubble, 8 to 10 minutes. Remove the pan from the heat and let rest for 3 hours, or until the oil becomes infused with the annatto.

2. Pour the oil slowly into a glass container and discard the sediment at the bottom of the saucepan. Cover tightly and store in the refrigerator for up to 2 weeks.

ANISE-VANILLA OIL

Makes about 2 cups

I had a wonderful dish in Peru that was flavored with anise and vanilla, which gave me the idea for this infused oil.

2 cups vegetable oil
25 pieces star anise
3 cloves
3 vanilla beans, split and scraped

1. Combine all the ingredients in a medium-size saucepan and heat over medium heat for 10 minutes to infuse the flavors. Remove from the heat to cool.

2. Do not strain. Use at once or store in an airtight jar in the refrigerator.

LEMON OIL

Makes about 2 cups

I've used this versatile oil for years. It's good for dressing greens, marinating fish, and incorporating into mojos. I am sure that once you have tried it, you will find as many uses for it around the kitchen as I have.

2 cups vegetable oil
¹/₄ cup lemon zest
2 teaspoons ground turmeric

1. Combine the oil, lemon zest, and turmeric in a saucepan and gently heat over low heat for 1 hour to infuse the oil with the lemon flavor.

2. Cool the oil and transfer to a squirt bottle. Use at once or store in the refrigerator for up to 2 weeks.

RED CHILE OIL

Makes about 2 cups

The annatto seeds will deepen the red color, but they won't change the rich flavor of the chiles. For a variation, substitute smoked chiles, such as chipotle or smoked chile pasilla de Oaxaca.

2 cups vegetable oil
2 tablespoons annatto seeds (optional, for color)
24 chiles d'arbol, stems removed
1 teaspoon kosher salt

1. Combine the oil, annatto seeds, chiles, and salt in a medium-size saucepan over medium-low heat. Gently heat for 15 to 20 minutes, being careful not to burn the chiles. Strain the oil into a container to cool. Discard the solids.

2. Transfer the cooled oil to a squirt bottle. Use at once or store in the refrigerator for up to 2 weeks.

GARLIC OIL

Makes 2 cups

This is one of those basics I couldn't live without because it's so easy and adds so much flavor.

15 garlic cloves
2 cups vegetable oil

1. In a medium saucepan, heat the garlic and oil over low heat until gently simmering. Continue to cook for 10 to 15 minutes, until the garlic is light golden and the oil is aromatic. Remove from the heat and let cool to room temperature. Remove and discard the garlic.

2. Use at once or store in the refrigerator for up to 2 weeks.

MOLE RUB

Makes about 1¹/₃ cups

The goal for moles is to achieve balance and complexity by harmoniously combining flavors, such as chiles, sweet plantains, caramelized onions, prunes, nuts, spices, and about fifteen other ingredients, including chocolate.

¹/₄ cup cocoa powder
¹/₄ cup powdered sugar
¹/₄ cup salt
2 tablespoons sesame seeds, toasted
2 tablespoons finely ground roasted peanuts
1 tablespoon ground pepper
1 tablespoon ground New Mexican red chile

1 tablespoon ground ancho chile
1 tablespoon ground chipotle chile
1 teaspoon ground ginger
1 teaspoon ground star anise
1 teaspoon ground cinnamon
¹/₄ teaspoon ground cloves
1¹/₂ teaspoons ground coriander
¹/₂ teaspoon ground dried oregano
¹/₂ teaspoon ground dried marjoram
¹/₄ teaspoon ground allspice

1. Thoroughly mix together all the ingredients.

2. Use at once or store in an airtight jar at room temperature.

BARBECUE SPICE RUB

Makes about 3¹/₂ cups

Be sure to keep this on hand for seasoning everything from chicken to steaks. It even makes a great coating for potato chips. When applied to meat, fish, or chicken the night before, the salt and sugar content draws out moisture while infusing flavor—essentially curing the food.

1 cup Spanish paprika
¹/₂ cup ground ancho chile
¹/₂ cup kosher salt
¹/₄ cup ground chipotle chile
¹/₄ cup firmly packed light brown sugar
¹/₄ cup granulated sugar
¹/₄ cup granulated garlic
¹/₄ cup granulated onion
¹/₄ cup freshly ground black pepper
2 tablespoons ground cumin

1. Thoroughly mix together all the ingredients.

2. Use at once or store in an airtight jar at room temperature for up to 6 months.

RUBS RUBS RUBS

ADOBOS, GLAZES, & VINAIGRETTES

FISH ADOBO

Makes about 1¹/₈ cups

This is basically a pickling spice rub that works well with fish. We like it best on shrimp and lobster. It enhances their flavor tremendously.

¹/₄ cup dill seeds

3 tablespoons coriander seeds

1 tablespoon ground allspice

4 whole cloves

3 tablespoons coarsely ground black pepper

2 tablespoons Colman's mustard powder

2 tablespoons ground ginger

6 dried bay leaves

1. In a medium-size sauté pan over medium heat, toast the dill seeds, coriander, allspice, and cloves until the aroma begins to release, about 3 minutes, and let cool.

2. Place the toasted spices in a large mortar and pound to a fine powder. Add the pepper, mustard powder, ginger, and bay leaves and mix well.

3. Use at once or store in an airtight jar for up to 6 months.

ORANGE-CORIANDER ADOBO

Makes about 1¹/₄ cups

A coffee grinder—used only for spices—makes a great spice mill for recipes like this one. Duck breast is the first thing that comes to mind for this adobo; however, scallops and shrimp work well, too. We like to rub it on skinless duck breasts, 2 to 3 hours before grilling. It is also great rubbed on partially cooked spareribs—use a generous amount.

¹/₄ cup coriander seeds

1 tablespoon mustard seeds

1 tablespoon cumin seeds

1 tablespoon aniseeds

3 tablespoons minced dried orange peel

3 tablespoons sugar

2 tablespoons salt

1 tablespoon dried oregano leaves

1 tablespoon cracked black pepper

Zest of 2 oranges, grated

1. In a skillet over medium heat, toast the coriander, mustard, cumin, and aniseeds until they are nutty and fragrant and begin to snap and crackle. Remove from the heat and allow to cool.

2. In a spice grinder, grind all the seeds and the orange peel.

3. Mix the ground seeds and peel, sugar, salt, oregano, pepper, and fresh zest in a bowl and cool.

4. Use at once or store in the refrigerator for up to 2 weeks.

DRIED MUSHROOM ADOBO

Makes about 1¹/₈ cups

You'd think the earthy flavor of mushrooms would dominate in this rub, but they don't. Instead, the mushroom flavor transforms the spices into a sweet, rich mix that is hard to classify. I like using it to coat white meat chicken, chayote, and scallops.

¹/₄ cup ground dried porcini mushrooms

¹/₄ cup sugar

3 tablespoons kosher salt

2 tablespoons ground coriander

2 tablespoons paprika

1 tablespoon coarsely ground black pepper

1 tablespoon ground chipotle chile

1 tablespoon Colman's mustard powder

1 teaspoon ground nutmeg

1 teaspoon ground aniseeds

1. Thoroughly mix together all the ingredients in a bowl.

2. Use at once or transfer to an airtight jar and store for up to 6 months.

ALIÑO ADOBO CRIOLLO

Makes about 1²/₃ cups

In Ecuador they have roadside kiosks lining the highways where roasted whole pigs and guinea pigs are sold. The guinea pigs are not so appetizing, but the pork is something else. This is a classical Ecuadorian marinade for pork. If you are going for a whole suckling pig, it is best to marinate it overnight.

¹/₂ cup ground annatto seeds

¹/₄ cup Spanish paprika

2 tablespoons garlic powder

3 tablespoons dried oregano

3 tablespoons kosher salt

2 tablespoons ground cumin

2 tablespoons ground dried lemon zest

2 tablespoons dried thyme

1. Thoroughly mix together all the ingredients.

2. Use at once or store in an airtight jar for up to 6 months.

CHIPOTLE–RED WINE ADOBO

Makes 3¹/₄ cups

This adobo is wet. I prefer to use it on larger, tougher cuts of meat, such as leg of lamb, beef sirloin, and pork butt. It also works fabulously on turkey breast and drumsticks.

1 (7-ounce) can chipotles in adobo
6 cloves garlic
1 tablespoon cumin seeds
1 cup diced Spanish onion
3 cups red Rioja wine
2 tablespoons celery seeds
6 sprigs rosemary
Leaves from 1 bunch thyme
2 tablespoons salt

1. Combine all the ingredients in a blender and purée.

2. Use at once or transfer to an airtight jar and store in the refrigerator for up to 2 weeks.

GARLIC-LEMON-BEER ADOBO

Makes about 5 cups

This wet adobo is a knock-out on turkey breast or chicken. I didn't invent this recipe; it's a traditional adobo made with chicha de jora—*Peruvian corn beer. But since chicha is hard to get, you may want to substitute regular dark beer.*

1 cup roasted garlic cloves (page 179)
Juice and zest of 4 lemons
12 ounces chicha de jora or dark beer
3 tablespoons honey
2 tablespoons ground ancho chile
1 cup fresh cilantro leaves
1 cup fresh dill leaves

1. Combine all the ingredients in a blender and purée.

2. Use at once or transfer to an airtight jar and store in the refrigerator for up to 2 weeks.

ADOBO ADOBO ADOBO

ROSEMARY-HONEY-MUSTARD ADOBO

Makes about 1 cup

I have used this adobo on lamb and goat. I've always particularly liked its flavor. I use it on tougher cuts, like leg and shank.

2 tablespoons black mustard seeds

2 tablespoons yellow mustard seeds

1 tablespoon coriander seeds

1 tablespoon white peppercorns

3 tablespoons dried rosemary

3 tablespoons kosher salt

1 tablespoon Colman's mustard powder

$1/4$ cup honey

1. In medium-size skillet over high heat, toast the mustard seeds, coriander, and peppercorns, turning often until they begin to smell fragrant. Remove from the heat and let them cool.

2. Combine the toasted spices in a spice grinder and pulse until they turn to powder.

3. Transfer the spice powder to a small bowl and mix in the rosemary, salt, mustard powder, and honey.

4. Use at once or transfer to an airtight jar and store in the refrigerator for up to 2 weeks.

PANELA RUM ADOBO

Makes about 4 cups

Panela is raw cane sugar, and its flavor blends well with rum, the liquid base for this traditional Venezuelan marinade. It is used to make asado negro (literally "black roast")—it turns the outside of the meat black. It is great on chicken and pork and tastes best when made 24 hours ahead of time.

2 cups dark rum

1 pound panela, grated, or 2 cups brown sugar plus $1/2$ cup molasses

2 tablespoons grated fresh ginger

8 cloves garlic

2 tablespoons ground star anise

3 tablespoons ground cinnamon

2 tablespoons coarsely ground black pepper

$1/2$ cup soy sauce

3 teaspoons Worcestershire sauce

1. Combine all the ingredients in a blender. Blend at high speed for about 30 seconds, until smooth.

2. Use at once or transfer to an airtight container and store in the refrigerator for up to 2 weeks.

ADOBO

JUNIPER BERRY–BAY LEAF RUM MARINADE

Makes 4 cups

This marinade has strong flavors that mellow the strong flavor of mature goat. I only cook with young goat, but I usually use a bit of this marinade for it.

3 cups dark rum
6 tablespoons juniper berries
6 bay leaves
4 sprigs rosemary
2 teaspoons ground cumin
2 teaspoons ground coriander
$1/4$ teaspoon ground nutmeg
6 tablespoons extra virgin olive oil
4 teaspoons salt
2 tablespoons packed brown sugar

1. Combine all the ingredients in a blender and purée.

2. Use at once or transfer to an airtight container and store in the refrigerator for up to 2 weeks.

RAIN FOREST GLAZE

Makes about 3$1/2$ cups

This recipe was invented by Jorge Adriazola, who is from Peru and one of my sous chefs. Since most of the ingredients came from the Amazon, Jorge called it Rain Forest Glaze. It pairs very well with pork, ribs, and duck. I would even attempt to use it on shrimp.

$1/4$ cup passion fruit purée
1 cup fresh or canned pineapple juice
1 cup cranberry juice
1 cup canned mango juice
Juice of 2 limes
$1 1/4$ teaspoons minced fresh ginger
$1/2$ habanero chile, seeded and chopped
  (for a hotter sauce, leave seeds in)
1 tablespoon sugar
1 teaspoon salt
1 teaspoon grated lemon zest
1 teaspoon grated orange zest
1 tablespoon cornstarch
1 tablespoon water
$1/4$ cup thinly sliced scallions, white and green parts

1. Prepare the glaze by combining passion fruit purée, pineapple juice, cranberry juice, mango juice, lime juice, ginger, chile, sugar, salt, and lemon and orange zest in a medium-size nonreactive saucepan. Bring to a boil and reduce by half.

2. Lower the heat to a simmer. Mix the cornstarch with the water and slowly pour it into the reduced glaze while stirring continuously. Add the scallions to the thickened glaze and remove from the heat.

3. Use at once or transfer to an airtight container and store in the refrigerator for up to 2 weeks.

COSTA RICAN COFFEE GLAZE

Makes 3 cups

Sounds nuts, but it works very well! Try it on pork.

3 tablespoons Anise-Vanilla Oil (page 150)

1 cup diced white onion

2 tablespoons grated fresh ginger

2 serrano chiles with seeds, diced

4 cloves garlic, chopped

3 tablespoons light molasses

1 cup dark rum

2 tablespoons ground coffee

1 tablespoon cocoa powder

1 tablespoon ground cinnamon

8 cups brewed coffee

3 tablespoons butter, softened to room temperature

Salt

1. In a medium-size sauté pan over high heat, heat the oil. Add the onion and sauté until caramelized, about 5 minutes. Add the ginger, chiles, and garlic. Continue to cook for about 3 minutes, then add the molasses.

2. Remove from the heat and add the rum, being careful that it does not flare up. Stir and cook for about 2 minutes. Add the ground coffee, cocoa, cinnamon, and 2 cups of the brewed coffee. Reduce the liquid by half and again add 2 cups of the brewed coffee. Reduce by half again and add the remaining 4 cups coffee. When the liquid is reduced to 3 cups, take the pan off the heat and let cool.

3. Purée in a blender and swirl in the butter. Add salt to taste.

4. Use at once or transfer to an airtight container and store in the refrigerator for up to 2 weeks.

TAMARIND-RUM-SOY GLAZE

Makes about 2^1/$_2$ cups

The flavors of vanilla and tamarind are just meant to be together! At the restaurant, we often pair these flavors in sorbets and sauces. There are several different tamarind products on the market, and they can usually be found in Asian groceries. Fresh tamarind is best, but may be difficult to find. We particularly like this glaze on smoked marlin.

4 ounces tamarind pulp, broken into pieces

^{3}/$_4$ cup dark rum

^{1}/$_4$ cup water

^{1}/$_2$ cup soy sauce

2 teaspoons kosher salt

^{1}/$_4$ cup light molasses

^{1}/$_4$ cup packed light brown sugar

1 tablespoon allspice berries

1^1/$_2$ teaspoons ground chipotle chiles

2 pieces star anise

1 vanilla bean, scraped

1. In a medium-size saucepan, soak the tamarind pulp in the rum and water for about 1 hour. Place the saucepan over a very low heat and cook for 30 minutes, stirring often.

2. Strain the mixture and discard the solids. Return the liquid to the saucepan and add the soy sauce, salt, molasses, brown sugar, allspice, ground chipotles, star anise, and vanilla bean. Over high heat, stir and cook for 5 minutes. Remove from the heat and cool to room temperature.

3. Use at once or transfer to an airtight container and store in the refrigerator for up to 2 weeks.

RED PEPPER VINAIGRETTE

Makes about 3/4 cup

If you are looking for plenty of flavor and no fat, here is the vinaigrette for you. We use it for all salad greens and green veggies, such as broccoli and green beans. You can substitute yellow bell pepper juice for a variation. You do need a vegetable juice extractor to make this vinaigrette.

3 red bell peppers
1/2 cup distilled white vinegar
1 bay leaf
1 tablespoon honey
1/2 teaspoon crushed red pepper flakes
1 teaspoon Thai fish sauce
Salt

1. Juice the red bell peppers in a juice extractor to obtain about 1/2 cup juice and reserve in the refrigerator.

2. Meanwhile, combine the vinegar, bay leaf, honey, and red pepper flakes in a saucepan. Over medium heat, reduce to half, stirring constantly. Cool and remove the bay leaf. Add the red pepper juice and fish sauce. Season with salt.

3. Use or once or transfer to an airtight jar and store in the refrigerator for up to 2 weeks.

GINGER VINAIGRETTE

Makes about 1 1/2 cups

When I do a special that includes coconut milk, I often include a salad dressed with this vinaigrette, which counterbalances the creaminess of the coconut. It is also great with tuna, swordfish, and chicken breasts.

1/4 cup Lemon Oil (page 150)
2 tablespoons minced garlic
2 tablespoons ginger juice
1/4 cup freshly squeezed lemon juice
2 tablespoons distilled white vinegar
5 scallions, green part only, finely sliced
1/4 cup loosely packed, coarsely chopped cilantro leaves
2 tablespoons sugar
Salt and freshly ground black pepper

1. Heat the lemon oil in a sauté pan over medium heat. Add the garlic and sauté until light golden, about 3 minutes.

2. Scrape into a bowl and mix in the ginger juice, lemon juice, vinegar, scallions, cilantro, and sugar. Season with salt and pepper.

3. Use at once or store in an airtight jar in the refrigerator for up to 1 week.

AJIS

GRILLED PINEAPPLE AJI

Makes about 2¹/₂ cups

Like many great dishes, this was created out of our constant need for resourcefulness. One week we had a ton of grilled pineapple left over, so we turned it into this fancy aji. It is fantastic paired with ham steak.

1 ripe pineapple, peeled and cut into ¹/₂- to 2-inch slices

3 tablespoons plus ¹/₄ cup Lemon Oil (page 150)

3 tablespoons sugar

1 tablespoon ground chipotle chiles

1 tablespoon kosher salt

¹/₂ cup diced white onion

3 cloves garlic, chopped

6 aji amarillo, seeded and stemmed

3 yellow tomatoes, diced (about 1 cup)

1 cup distilled white vinegar

¹/₂ cup pineapple juice

1 tablespoon turmeric powder

¹/₄ cup light rum

Salt

1. Prepare a hot fire in the grill.

2. In a bowl, toss the pineapple slices with the 3 tablespoons oil, sugar, chipotle powder, and kosher salt.

3. Arrange the pineapple slices on the hot grate and grill for about 3 minutes per side, until golden brown. Remove from the grill and let cool. Remove the core, dice the meat, and reserve.

4. In a large saucepan over high heat, heat the remaining ¹/₄ cup lemon oil. Add the onion, garlic, aji amarillo, and tomatoes and sauté for about 4 minutes. Then add the vinegar, pineapple juice, turmeric, and rum. Reduce to a simmer, cover, and cook for about 30 minutes.

4. Stir in the grilled pineapple and let it rest for about 10 minutes. Then add salt to taste and purée in a blender.

5. Use at once or store in an airtight jar in the refrigerator for up to 4 days.

OPAL BASIL CHIMICHURRI

Makes 1¹/₂ to 2 cups

Chimichurri is a pestolike condiment from Argentina, classically made with parsley, garlic, and olive oil.

2 fresh lime leaves, stemmed
  (substitute Kaffir lime leaves)

2 dried bay leaves

1 tablespoon celery seeds

4 shallots, diced

2 cloves garlic, diced

1 tablespoon kosher salt

2 bunches coarsely chopped, loosely packed opal basil

¹/₂ cup coarsely chopped, loosely packed oregano

¹/₂ cup virgin olive oil

¹/₄ cup red wine vinegar

1. Combine the lime leaves, bay leaves, celery seeds, shallots, garlic, and salt in a mortar and work into a smooth paste.

2. In a bowl, combine the paste from the mortar with the chopped basil and oregano, oil, and vinegar and mix well.

3. Refrigerate, then serve chilled or store in the refrigerator for up to 2 days.

HUACATAY AJÍ

Makes about 2 cups

Huacatay is a black mint from Peru. It is widely used in the Peruvian kitchen in the region of Arequipa. It has a definite flavor, which you can merely approximate by substituting fresh mint mixed with a leaf or two of cilantro. This is the aji used in one of my signature dishes, Oysters Rodriguez.

1/2 cup fresh cilantro leaves, picked over
2 cups fresh huacatay leaves (substitute mint)
6 cloves garlic
1/2 cup cachucha peppers (aji dulce), stemmed
1/2 cup diced red onion
4 jalapeño peppers, diced with the seeds
1/2 cup freshly squeezed lime juice
1/2 cup olive oil
1/2 cup loosely packed crumbled feta cheese
Salt

1. Combine all the ingredients in a blender, adding salt to taste. Pulse a few times. Then blend on full speed for about 40 seconds.

2. Refrigerate, then serve chilled or store in the refrigerator for up to 1 week.

PEBRE

Makes about 2 cups

My father's wife, Erika, is from Chile. On a trip to Chile, her family introduced me to this traditional Chilean condiment. It is used for everything—from a dip for bread to a hot sauce for soup. Using the mortar is important because, unlike a food processor or blender, it produces a paste rather than a purée.

Leaves from 3 sprigs fresh oregano
3 ripe red jalapeño peppers, minced
2 cloves garlic, minced
1/2 red bell pepper, minced
1 teaspoon salt
1/4 cup red wine vinegar
2 tablespoons olive oil
12 ounces ripe plum tomatoes,
   peeled, seeded, and diced
1/4 cup fresh cilantro, minced
1/2 red onion, minced
5 scallions, thinly sliced

1. In a large mortar, combine the oregano, jalapeños, garlic, bell pepper, and salt. Work into a paste.

2. In a large bowl, mix the vinegar and oil with a whisk and blend well. Add the paste from the mortar, the tomatoes, cilantro, onion, and scallions. Mix well.

3. Refrigerate, then serve chilled or store in the refrigerator for up to 2 days.

CULANTRO AJI

Makes about 2 cups

When I returned from a trip to Ecuador, where I had explored the many uses of culantro, I tried desperately to locate the cilantro-like herb in the states. No one knew of it as culantro, but one of my produce vendors explained that it was called "recao" in Puerto Rico and "shadow benny" in Jamaica. Now that culantro is finally available to me in New York City, Latin grocers should be able to stock it for home cooks.

1 pound recao, washed, stemmed, and chopped
6 cloves garlic, chopped
1 cup cachucha peppers (aji dulce), stemmed
1 cup fresh flat-leaf parsley, packed
3 jalapeño peppers, seeded and chopped
1/2 cup thinly sliced scallions, green parts only
1/2 cup olive oil
Juice of 3 limes
1/2 cup water

1. Combine all the ingredients in a blender and purée until smooth.

2. Refrigerate, then serve chilled or store in the refrigerator for up to 2 days.

ROCOTO AJI

Makes about 1 1/2 cups

This sweet-and-sour sauce reminds us a lot of a Thai-style sauce and goes very well with shrimp, scallops, chicken, and turkey. Rocoto chiles, also known as rocotillos, are orangey yellow or bright red, small, and roundly squat like pattypan squash. They are related to habaneros and Scotch bonnets, and hence share those chiles' fruitiness and intense heat.

8 rocoto chiles, seeded and finely diced
   (substitute red jalapeños or Fresno chiles)
2 red bell peppers, diced
1 cup distilled white vinegar
2 tablespoons sugar
2 tablespoons salt
4 cloves garlic, finely chopped
1 1/2 tablespoons honey
1 tablespoon cornstarch mixed
   with 2 tablespoons water

1. In a medium-size saucepan, combine the rocoto chiles, bell peppers, vinegar, sugar, salt, garlic, and honey. Bring to a simmer and simmer for about 5 minutes. Add the cornstarch mixture and stir well. Over medium heat, cook for about 5 minutes longer, then remove from the heat and let cool.

2. Refrigerate, then serve chilled or store in the refrigerator for up to 1 week.

SALSAS, MOJOS, & MISCELLANEA

OVEN-DRIED TOMATO AND FENNEL SALSA

Makes about 3 cups

This could be the start of a new fusion cuisine. We call it "Latino Italiano." Spoon it over grilled steak or grilled Italian sausage.

8 ripe plum tomatoes

Salt

1 cup finely diced fennel

2 red onions, finely diced

3 cloves garlic, finely chopped

1/2 cup fresh basil leaves, picked from stem and julienned

2 tablespoons fresh oregano leaves, picked from stem

1 teaspoon crushed red pepper flakes

2/3 cup extra virgin olive oil

1/3 cup aged red wine vinegar

1/2 cup toasted pine nuts (page 179)

1. Preheat the oven to 200°F. Cut the tomatoes in half lengthwise and place on a wire rack sitting on a sheet pan. Sprinkle with a little salt (which extracts the excess juices) and place them cut side down in the warm oven overnight. The tomatoes should shrink and wrinkle and have the texture of dried prunes. This step can be done well in advance. Store the dried tomatoes in resealable bags or in glass jars covered in olive oil.

2. To make the salsa, dice the oven-dried tomatoes and toss with the fennel, onions, garlic, basil, oregano, red pepper flakes, olive oil, vinegar, and pine nuts.

3. Serve chilled or at room temperature. Store leftovers in an airtight container in the refrigerator for up to 2 weeks.

SALSAS & MOJOS & SALSAS & MOJOS & SALSAS

SUNCHOKE SALSA

Makes about 2 cups

As always, we try to use as many parts of the foods we cook with as possible.

1 cup water

1 cup distilled white vinegar

1 cup dry white wine

1 teaspoon salt

8 ounces sunchokes, washed and peeled

2 tablespoons plus 1 teaspoon sunflower oil

3 tablespoons chopped shallots

1 small red onion, finely diced

1/4 cup minced chives

2 tablespoons chopped roasted garlic (page 179)

1 long red hot pepper, sliced thinly crosswise

1 (3.5-ounce) package sunflower sprouts, washed and trimmed

1/4 cup toasted sunflower seeds (page 179)

2 tablespoons champagne vinegar

2 tablespoons chopped fresh chervil

Kosher salt and freshly ground black pepper

1. Bring the water, vinegar, wine, and salt to a boil. Add the sunchokes and blanch for about 5 minutes, until tender, but firm. Refresh under cold water. When cool enough to handle, slice them into thin rounds.

2. In a small skillet over medium-high heat, heat the 1 teaspoon sunflower oil. Add the shallots and sauté until translucent, about 3 minutes.

3. In a nonreactive bowl, combine the sunchokes, shallots, remaining 2 tablespoons oil, onion, chives, garlic, hot pepper, sunflower sprouts, sunflower seeds, vinegar, chervil, and salt and pepper.

4. Serve chilled or at room temperature. Store leftovers in an airtight container in the refrigerator for up to 1 week.

BANANA-LIME SALSA

Makes about 2 cups

This simple salsa gives a burst of tropical flavor to grilled duck breast, squab, or any other game bird, especially when paired with the rich demiglace of the respective bird. It's also a good match for seafood.

6 ripe, firm yellow bananas, cut into 1/4-inch dice

6 limes, segmented and segments cut in half

2 tablespoons honey

2 tablespoons fresh mint leaves, roughly chopped

1. In a nonreactive bowl, gently mix all ingredients together.

2. Serve warm or at room temperature. Store leftovers in an airtight container in the refrigerator for up to 1 week, bringing the salsa to room temperature before serving.

Smoky Corn Salsa

Makes 2 cups

Rubbing a little oil on the outside of the ears of corn helps the smoke permeate to the kernels, and they will retain that smoky flavor longer. This salsa complements just about anything. It is great cold, but we prefer to serve it warm from the grill.

1 red bell pepper
1 green bell pepper
3 whole scallions, trimmed
3 ears yellow sweet corn, unshucked and lightly oiled
1 generous tablespoon Annatto Oil (page 150)
1 tablespoon chopped cilantro
Juice of 1 lime
Salt and freshly ground black pepper

1. Prepare a medium fire in the grill. Cover 2 or 3 handfuls of hickory or mesquite chips with water and set aside to soak.

2. When the coals are glowing with white ash, place the peppers on the grill and char on all sides until evenly blackened. Transfer to a bowl, cover with plastic wrap, and set aside. Place the scallions on the grill for 2 to 3 minutes on each side, until lightly charred. Transfer the scallions to a small bowl and set aside.

3. Add the soaked wood chips to the fire. Then place the corn on the grill, cover the grill, and smoke the corn for 15 minutes. Turn and smoke the other side for another 10 minutes. Place on a plate to cool.

4. Peel, seed, and dice the peppers into $1/4$-inch pieces. Dice the scallions into $1/4$-inch pieces. Combine in a bowl. Shuck the corn and remove the corn silks. Hold an ear of corn so it is standing on a cutting board and, with a sharp knife, slice away the smoked corn kernels from the cob. Add the corn to the peppers, along with the chipotle oil, cilantro, lime juice, and salt and pepper.

5. Serve warm or chilled. Store leftovers in an airtight container in the refrigerator for up to 4 days.

Seven Lily Salsa

Makes about 2$1/2$ cups

Combining the seven lilies—that is, seven members of the onion family—is a perennial favorite for me. Serve this salsa alongside everything that you would usually serve with raw onion, such as beef, steak, pork, and grilled fish or chicken.

1 small white onion, peeled
1 red onion, peeled
$1/2$ cup thinly sliced scallions, green and white parts
1 bunch chives
2 cups oil
2 leeks, white parts only, trimmed and julienned
Salt and freshly ground black pepper
Onion sprouts (substitute alfalfa sprouts)
Juice of 1 lemon
2 tablespoons Garlic Oil (page 151)

1. Cut the white onion in half and place cut side down on a cutting board. Cut crosswise into very thin half-moon slices. Repeat with the other half and do the same with the red onion. Trim the root ends of the scallions and thinly slice with a slight diagonal slant. Combine the red and white onions and scallions in a bowl. Cut the chives into 1-inch pieces and add to the rest of the onions.

2. In a medium-sized pot, heat the oil to 350°F.

3. Fry the leeks in the hot oil until crisp, about 1 to 2 minutes. Remove and drain on paper towels. Season with salt and pepper and add to the onion mixture together with the onion sprouts.

4. Dress with lemon juice and garlic oil, and serve at once.

5. The salsa may be stored undressed in an airtight container in the refrigerator for up to 2 days.

MANGO-MUSTARD SALSA

Makes about 2¹/₂ cups

This salsa is simply delicious with grilled salmon, scallops, shrimp, grilled sliced chicken breast, and pork loin chops.

2 ripe mangoes, peeled and cut into ¹/₄-inch dice

¹/₂ cup thinly bias-sliced scallions, green parts only

1 red bell pepper, seeded and cut into ¹/₄-inch dice

2 tablespoons American-style yellow mustard

1 teaspoon black mustard seeds

2 tablespoons white wine vinegar

2 tablespoons mustard oil

2 tablespoons coarsely chopped fresh cilantro

Juice of 2 limes

1 jalapeño chile, minced

1. Combine all the ingredients in a nonreactive bowl and mix well.

2. Refrigerate until ready to serve or transfer to an airtight container and store in the refrigerator for up to 2 weeks.

BACALAO-CAPER SALSA

Makes about 2 cups

Serve this salsa with some crusty Cuban (or any other) bread on a warm day. Spooned onto crisp tostones (refried flattened plantains), it makes a terrific hors d'oeuvre.

1 pound bacalao (dried salt cod)

1 ounce caperberries, stems removed and sliced into thin rounds

1 ounce nonpareil capers

¹/₄ cup pitted imported black olives, sliced into rounds

1 red bell pepper, cut into ¹/₈-inch dice

1 medium red onion, cut into ¹/₈-inch dice

2 medium red tomatoes, cut into ¹/₄-inch dice

2 cloves garlic, finely minced

¹/₂ cup coarsely chopped parsley

¹/₂ teaspoon crushed red pepper flakes

¹/₂ cup olive oil

Juice of 2 lemons

Freshly ground black pepper

1. Soak the bacalao in cold water overnight in the refrigerator. The next day, rinse the cod and place in a pot with fresh water. Bring the water to a boil and boil gently for 1 hour. The degree of saltiness can fluctuate with less or more soaking and boiling time. Once the bacalao is cool enough to handle, shred it into medium to small flakes, taking care not to shred it so finely that it resembles a paste.

2. Toss the salt cod with the caperberries, capers, olives, bell pepper, onion, tomatoes, garlic, parsley, red pepper flakes, olive oil, and lemon juice. Add black pepper to taste. (Seasoning with salt is unnecessary because the fish, as well as the capers, are salty.)

3. Serve at room temperature or chilled. Store leftovers in an airtight container in the refrigerator for up to 1 week.

SHALLOT-TRUFFLE MOJO

Makes about 2¹/₂ cups

If you order a chef-inspired tasting menu at my restaurant, you will most likely see this mojo appear on one course. It is one of those simple, but very versatile, mojos that complements a wide range of food, including oysters, scallops, salmon, poultry, and any salad with potato or green beans.

8 ounces dried black trumpet mushrooms
12 shallots, finely minced
¹/₂ cup champagne vinegar
¹/₂ cup white truffle oil
Salt and freshly ground black pepper

1. Place the mushrooms in a bowl, cover with warm water, and let soak for about 1 hour, until softened. Using your hands, take all whole trumpets and tear them in half lengthwise to make sure there is no sand or dirt trapped in the narrow part of the trumpets. Place them in a colander under cold running water, vigorously rinse, drain, and place them on a clean towel to absorb excess moisture. Then finely mince the trumpets.

2. Combine the mushrooms in a bowl with the shallots, vinegar, and truffle oil. Season to taste with salt and pepper.

3. Serve at room temperature. Store in an airtight container in the refrigerator for up to 2 weeks.

MINT MOJO

Makes 1¹/₂ cups

Whenever I do a lamb special, I like to include this mojo in the dish. Let's face it, lamb and mint are a great combo! This Latinized mint jelly mojo awakens memories, as well as the flavor of lamb. It is also a great match for grilled vegetables.

1 cup distilled white vinegar
2 tablespoons mint jelly
1 cup tightly packed fresh mint leaves, stemmed and finely chopped
5 shallots, minced
2 cloves garlic, minced
1 jalapeño chile, seeded and minced
2 tablespoons vegetable oil
Salt and freshly ground black pepper

1. In a saucepan, combine the vinegar and mint jelly. Boil until the mixture is reduced by half. Cool completely.

2. Add the mint, shallots, garlic, jalapeño, and vegetable oil. Season to taste with salt and pepper.

3. Serve chilled. Store leftovers in an airtight container in the refrigerator for up to 5 days.

PASSION FRUIT MOJO

Makes about 1 cup

Add a summery tropical touch to your barbecue by using this mojo on any fish or chicken hot off the grill.

4 ounces fresh-ripened passion fruit pulp with seeds
2 ounces frozen passion fruit purée
2 tablespoons finely minced shallots
2 tablespoons chives, minced
2 tablespoons chopped cilantro
Juice of 4 limes
6 tablespoons olive oil
Salt and freshly ground black pepper

1. In a stainless steel bowl, mix together the passion fruit pulp, passion fruit purée, shallots, chives, cilantro, and lime juice.

2. Add the oil in one long steady stream, while whisking with a wire whip until emulsified. Season with salt and pepper to taste.

3. Serve chilled. Store leftovers in an airtight container in the refrigerator for up to 1 week.

STAR FRUIT MOJO

Makes about 2 cups

Star fruit, or carambola, are ripe and ready to eat when they are deep golden in color and their outer ridges darken. Their flavor is similar to a blend of apples and white grapes with a lemony tang, which makes them perfect in a light mojo for chicken breasts, tuna, and shrimp or as a unique dressing for greens. Their season is quite short, mainly limited to June and July. This mojo should be made just before it is served.

8 star fruit
4 scallions, green parts only, thinly sliced
1 small red onion, finely diced
$1/2$ habanero chile, finely minced
2 tablespoons chopped cilantro
1 tablespoon finely minced fresh lemon verbena
Juice of 4 limes
$1/4$ cup light vegetable oil
1 teaspoon honey
Pinch salt

1. Extract the juice from six of the star fruit and set aside. With a sharp knife, trim the brown edges from the remaining two and dice into $1/2$-inch pieces. You may wish to reserve two or three star-shaped slices for a garnish.

2. Blend all the ingredients together and serve at once. Store leftovers in an airtight container in the refrigerator for up to 1 day.

TOMATILLO-POBLANO MARMALADE

Makes 1 pint

This marmalade goes extremely well with any rare piece of meat. The juices that come out of the meat, together with the marmalade, make a wonderful combination

2 roasted poblano chiles (page 179), peeled and diced

1 jalapeño chile, finely chopped

8 cloves garlic, finely chopped

1¹/₂-inch piece ginger, peeled and finely chopped

1 cup sugar

1¹/₂ teaspoons kosher salt

¹/₂ cup water

20 tomatillos, peeled, washed, and quartered

1 bunch cilantro, leaves chopped

1. Combine the poblanos, jalapeno, garlic, ginger, sugar, salt, and water in a saucepan. Bring to boil, then lower the heat and simmer until thick and syrupy, about 30 minutes. Pour into a blender with the cilantro and purée until smooth.

2. Return the puréed sauce to the pan with the tomatillos and cook over medium-low heat, stirring, until the tomatillos are just cooked and the marmalade coats the back of a spoon, 20 to 30 minutes. Remove from the heat and set aside to cool.

3. Transfer the marmalade to an airtight container and refrigerate until chilled, then serve. Store leftovers in the refrigerator for up to 2 weeks.

HABANERO SAUCE

Makes about 1 quart

This sauce is for every chilehead. It goes on and with everything!

1 pound yellow habanero chiles, stemmed and chopped with seeds

1 pound yellow bell peppers, stemmed, seeded, and diced

1 cup diced Spanish onion

2 cups distilled white vinegar

8 cloves garlic, chopped

1 tablespoon ground turmeric

2 cups water

2 tablespoons Colman's mustard powder

1 cup American-style yellow mustard

¹/₂ cup peeled and grated fresh ginger

1. In a medium-size saucepan over medium heat, combine all the ingredients. Bring to a boil, lower the heat, cover, and simmer about 1 hour, until the chiles and peppers have softened. Remove from the heat and let cool for about 1 hour.

2. Pour half into the bowl of a food processor and purée. Transfer puréed portion to a bowl and purée the other half of the pepper mixture. Cover and refrigerate.

3. Serve at room temperature. Store in an airtight container in the refrigerator for up to 4 weeks.

SAFFRON–AJI AMARILLO SAUCE

Makes about 2¹/₂ cups

With its vibrant, electrifying yellow color, this aji looks great with just about anything that is charred. I keep it in the refrigerator in a squirt bottle and use it like mayonnaise on sandwiches.

6 cloves garlic, sliced

4 shallots, sliced

1 tablespoon saffron threads

2 jalapeño chiles, sliced

4 bay leaves

1 teaspoon black peppercorns

1 cup distilled white vinegar

1 cup white wine

2 cups mayonnaise

1 (6-ounce) jar Aji Amarillo Sauce
  (see Sources, page 183)

1 tablespoon salt

1. Combine the garlic, shallots, saffron, jalapeños, bay leaves, peppercorns, vinegar, and wine in a small saucepan. Reduce over medium heat until ¹/₂ cup remains. Cool the reduction and remove the peppercorns and bay leaves.

2. In a blender or food processor, purée the reduction until smooth. In a bowl, mix the reduction with the mayonnaise and bottled aji amarillo sauce. Add the salt and mix well.

3. Serve at once. Store leftovers in an airtight container in the refrigerator for up to 2 weeks.

TAMARIND TARTAR SAUCE

Makes 1¹/₄ cups

If you like tartar sauce, you will love this unique version. I especially like it with any crispy coated fried fish. The tamarind supplies a complex touch of tang and sweetness to counterbalance the richness of the sour cream and mayonnaise, while accentuating the tartness of the capers and the saltiness of the olives.

¹/₄ cup pitted black olives

¹/₄ cup pitted green olives

1 tablespoon capers

¹/₄ cup tamarind pulp, seeds removed

¹/₄ cup sour cream

¹/₄ cup mayonnaise

1. In a food processor, combine the black and green olives and pulse to chop. Do not purée; leave them a little chunky. Transfer the olives to a bowl and add the capers, tamarind pulp, sour cream, and mayonnaise.

2. Refrigerate until you are ready to serve.

LOBSTER STOCK

Makes about 3 quarts

Home made stocks are one of the secrets of professional cooking. Once you make your own, you'll taste the difference and never want to use premade stocks again.

5 pounds lobster shells (or carcasses), split

1 cup butter

4 to 6 carrots, peeled and coarsely shopped

4 to 6 celery stalks

4 white onions, coarsely chopped

3 garlic cloves, halved

3 cups aged dry sherry

1 tablespoon crushed red pepper flakes

4 bay leaves

1 bunch thyme, tied into bundle with kitchen twine

1 bunch parsley, tied into bundle with kitchen twine

1/4 cup tomato paste

1 gallon water

1. Thoroughly rinse lobster shells and remove lungs.

2. Melt the butter in a large stockpot over medium-high heat. Add the lobster shells, carrots, celery, onions, and garlic, and saute, stirring continuously until softened, about 20 minutes. Add the wine and deglaze the pot. Cook 5 more minutes.

3. Add the remaining ingredients and bring to a boil. When the mixture is boiling, decrease the heat to low and simmer for 2 hours, periodically skimming off any fat and impurities that rise to the surface.

4. Strain the stock through a fine-mesh strainer. Discard the solids.

5. Use stock as directed, or transfer to airtight container(s) and refrigerate for up to 2 days or freeze for up to 2 months.

SIMPLE SYRUP

Makes 2 cups

Simple syrup is one of the elemental ingredients in many mixed drinks, dessert sauces, cakes, and other desserts. It gives them a silky sweetness without the grainy texture of uncoooked sugar.

1 cup granulated sugar

2 cups water

1. Place the sugar in a small saucepan. Slowly pour the water over the sugar. Place the pan over medium heat, stirring the sugar to dissolve, and bring to a boil. Let the syrup boil for 2 minutes. Remove from the heat and let cool to room temperature.

2. Use at once or transfer the syrup to a small jar and refrigerate for up to 2 weeks.

CHIPOTLE KETCHUP

Makes about 1 1/2 cups

This spicy, smoky substitute for ordinary ketchup is a staple at every grill party I give.

1/4 cup vegetable oil

2 onions, chopped

5 garlic cloves

1/2 cup aged sherry wine vinegar

3 tablespoons honey

1 (7-ounce) can chipotles in adobo

2 (16-ounce) cans tomato paste

3 tablespoons kosher salt

1. Preheat the oven to 350°F.

2. Heat the oil in a large oven-safe saucepan over medium heat. Add the onions and garlic and sauté for 10 minutes. Add the vinegar, honey, chipotles, tomato paste, and salt. Stir and cover with a lid.

3. Place in the oven for 45 minutes. Remove and let cool.

4. Transfer the ketchup to a food processor and purée until smooth. Or purée using a small immersion stick blender.

5. Serve chilled or at room temperature. Store leftovers in an airtight container in the refrigerator for up to 1 week.

PICKLED JALAPEÑOS

Makes 1 quart

You will never use jarred or canned pickled jalapeños again once you've had these. They're a snap to make, and they keep for 6 to 8 weeks in the refrigerator. They probably last longer, although we can never keep them around long enough to know for sure. Pickled jalapeños are a great addition to any sandwich and delicious tossed in a salsa or salad.

10 red jalapeño chiles, sliced into very thin rounds
10 green jalapeño chiles, sliced into very thin rounds
5 shallots, thinly sliced
5 cloves garlic, thinly sliced
2 cups distilled white vinegar
2 tablespoons sugar
2 tablespoons kosher salt
2 fresh bay leaves

1. Combine all the ingredients in a container, mix thoroughly, and cover with a lid.

2. "Cure" in the refrigerator for 24 hours, then serve. Once cured, the jalapeños may be stored in the refrigerator for up to 8 weeks.

SWEET CORN–SAFFRON SAUCE

Makes about 2 1/2 cups

The natural sweetness of the corn and unmistakable perfume of saffron is a great combination of flavors to go with lobster, scallops, or any vegetable plate.

12 ears corn, shucked
2 tablespoons butter
6 shallots, sliced
1 carrot, chopped
3 celery stalks, chopped
1 teaspoon saffron
2 quarts water
Salt

1. With a sharp knife, cut down the sides of the corn to remove the kernels. Reserve the cobs. Gather the kernels and pass through a juice extractor. Set the corn juice aside in the refrigerator. With a heavy sharp knife or cleaver, cut cobs in 2-inch pieces.

2. In a large pot, melt the butter over medium heat. Add the shallots, carrot, celery, and corncob pieces and sauté for 10 minutes. Add the saffron and sauté for another 2 minutes. Add the water and bring to a boil. Lower the heat and cook until the corn stock is reduced to 2 cups. Strain and reserve the liquid.

3. Combine the corn juice with the saffron-corn stock in a small pot and cook together until slightly thickened. Season with salt to taste and serve at once.

4. Store leftovers in an airtight container in the refrigerator for up to 4 days.

TOASTING
NUTS

TOASTING SPICES AND SEEDS

PEELING AND SEEDING TOMATOES

ROASTING
GARLIC

PEELING
PLANTAINS

ROASTING CHILES AND BELL PEPPERS

TECHNIQUES

PEELING AND SEEDING TOMATOES

Prepare an ice water bath. Bring a large saucepan of water to a boil. Drop in the whole tomatoes and blanch for 1 minute, then immediately transfer to the ice water bath. When cool enough to handle, peel the tomatoes, cut in half crosswise, and gently squeeze each half to remove the seeds. Use as directed.

PEELING PLANTAINS

Fill your sink with warm water. Cut off both ends of each plantain and make 3 or 4 lengthwise slits through the skin. Place the plantains in the water and soak for about 10 minutes, then peel by running your fingers under the skin.

ROASTING CHILES AND BELL PEPPERS

Place the chiles or peppers on the grill rack over a medium fire, hold suspended over a gas flame, or set on a baking sheet under a broiler. Roast until skins are blistered and blackened all over, but before flesh becomes charred. Transfer to a bowl and cover tightly with plastic wrap. Let steam for 10 to 15 minutes. When cool enough to handle, remove the skins with your fingers or the tip of a knife. Remove and discard the seeds (unless recipe instructs otherwise) and internal ribs, and use as directed. Warning: Do not touch your face or eyes after handling chiles until you have thoroughly washed your hands. If you have sensitive skin, wear rubber gloves when handling chiles.

ROASTING GARLIC

Slice about $1/4$ inch off the top of the head of garlic and discard. Place garlic on a square of foil and drizzle with olive oil. Wrap garlic in foil and roast in a 250°F oven until soft, about 40 to 50 minutes.

TOASTING NUTS

Place nuts on a baking sheet and toast in a 350°F oven for 7 to 10 minutes, until golden brown and aromatic. Let cool completely, then use as directed.

TOASTING SPICES AND SEEDS

Place the spices or seeds in a dry skillet over low heat. Toast, stirring frequently, for about 1 minute, until fragrant. Alternatively, place on a baking sheet and toast in a 350°F oven for 5 to 7 minutes, until fragrant.

GLOSSARY

This glossary is based on Spanish words and terms that refer to Latin American ingredients and foods. Keep in mind that some of the ingredient names will vary from country to country.

Achiote: Also known as annatto. Brick-red seeds of a tree native to the New World, with a mildly acidic, orangelike flavor. Used as a natural coloring to give a yellowish tint to foods, including butter and cheese.

Ancho: Dried form of the poblano chile. Has sweet, fruity tones and mild heat.

Boniato: Tuber also known as white sweet potato, Florida yam, and camote. It looks like a sweet potato on the outside, but is shorter and rounder and has white, sweetish, mealy flesh. The boniato is usually large, averaging 1 1/2 to 2 pounds. Scrub well before using.

Cachuca: Tiny, round chile also known as aji dulce. Usually green, with little heat but a pungent aroma and an acidic, slightly fruity flavor.

Calabaza: Also called the West Indian pumpkin. A large, round, sweet squash, resembling a pumpkin (for which it can be substituted) in its size and orange flesh. Firm texture and sweet flavor.

Chicha de jora: Beer made from corn, usually blue corn. Available in Latin American markets.

Chimichurri: Pestolike condiment from Argentina, traditionally served with churrasco. Made with a base of parsley, garlic, and olive oil.

Chorizo: Spicy Spanish hard pork sausage. Substitute salami. Not to be confused wth spicy Mexican chorizo, which is made with fresh pork and is sold in sausage, patty, or bulk form.

Churrasco: Argentinian dish of marinated and grilled skirt steak.

Coconut milk: Liquid prepared from the meat of fresh coconuts blended with water and strained (or heated and strained). It is most easily available canned.

Culantro: Type of cilantro with long, flat leaf. Also known as recao or culantrio.

Dende oil: Red, acidic oil extracted from palm nuts.

Epazote: Pungent Mexican herb available fresh and dried (use fresh if possible).

Hearts of palm: Also known as palmitos. Tender ivory-colored shoots of a type of palm. Available fresh and canned in Latin American and gourmet markets.

Huacatay: Black mint from Peru. Substitute fresh mint mixed with a leaf or two of cilantro.

Huitlacoche: Fungus that grow in the kernels of corn, making them morph into irregular-shaped gray-black mounds. Has earthy flavor often likened to mushrooms or truffles.

Malanga: Starchy root vegetable popular throughout Latin America and used much like a potato. Nutty, earthy flavor; the yellow-to-red flesh turns gray when cooked. Also known as yautia and taro.

Masa harina: Lime-processed, dried ground corn that's available in fine and coarse grinds.

Mojo: Spicy (not hot) sauce, particularly popular in Cuba, usually served with cooked foods. Typically made with garlic, citrus juice, oil, and at least one type of herb.

Pinton: A semiripe plantain.

Pisco: Peruvian grape liqueur similar to the Italian grappa.

Plantain: Plantano in Spanish. A member of the banana family that is always used cooked. Sweet bananalike flavor with a brownish black skin when ripe; starchy in flavor with yellow skin that's freckled or spotted when semiripe; green skin in unripe state.

Poblano: Fresh green chile especially popular in Mexico and Central America. In its dried form it's called the ancho chile.

Queso blanco: Salty, firm, white cheese similar to mozzarella or Muenster. Common in Latin American cooking and available in Latin American and gourmet markets.

Queso fresco: Soft, crumbly, mild white cheese similar to ricotta or farmer's cheese. Does not melt well.

Quinoa: (Pronounced KEEN-wah) A tiny, ancient grain-like seed, cultivated by the Incas that's still grown extensively in the Andean region of South America. High in protein and nutrients. Used like rice or couscous.

Scotch bonnet: Hot chile with fruity tones that's popular in the Caribbean. A close relative of the habanero, which is the hottest chile of all.

Sofrito: Mixture of puréed, sautéed, onions, garlic, and bell peppers, used as a flavoring base for soups, stews, and other dishes.

Tamarind: Popular Latin American legume, related to beans. Pods yield a pulp with a sweet and sour flavor. Tamarind is widely used in Latin America as a flavoring. Blocks of tamarind pulp or paste and tamarind juice, which comes in fresh and frozen form, are available at Latin American and Asian markets.

Yuca: Starchy root vegetable popular throughout Latin America. To peel the long, tubular roots, hold in one hand and make broad slashing motions down the tuber with a heavy-duty, large knife. (A regular vegetable peeler will not work.)

SOURCES FOR INGREDIENTS

Coyote Café General Store
132 West Water Street
Santa Fe, NM 87501
(800) 866-4695

Dried chiles, chipotles in adobo sauce, masa harina, chile powders and other spices

Dean & Deluca
560 Broadway
New York, NY 10012
(800) 221-7714
www.dean-deluca.com

Chile powders, dried chiles, beans, and quinoa

EthnicGrocer.com

Masa, chiles, hominy, beans, spices, and other Latin ingredients (including hearts of palm)

King Arthur Flour
PO Box 876
Norwich, VT 05055-0876
(800) 827–6836
www.KingArthurFlour.com

Flour, cocoa (including Van Leer), chocolate, vanilla and other baking ingredients and equipment

Melissa's Specialty Foods
PO Box 21127
Los Angeles, CA 90021
(800) 588-0151
www.melissas.com

Dried chiles, epazote, piloncillo, tamarind

Penzey's Spice House, Ltd.
PO Box 933
W19362 Apollo Drive
Muskego, WI 53150
(800) 741-7787
www.penzeys.com

Chile powders, dried chiles, and epazote

QueRico.com

Wide selection of ingredients from Mexico, Argentina, Brazil, and the Caribbean

ÏNDEX

Fin

ALSO FROM DOUGLAS RODRÍGUEZ

"Mr. Rodriguez's reinterpretations of Latin American dishes
have made him something of a godfather of contemporary Latin American cooking."

—Eric Asimov, *New York Times*, 1999

"Rodriguez has established himself as the mambo king of a new cuisine....
The food puts on a floor show."

—*People*

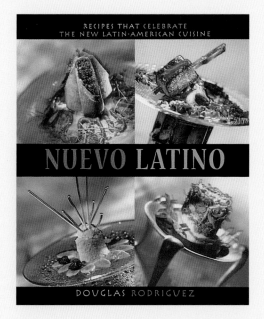

*Recipes that Celebrate
the New Latin American Cuisine*

$8\,^7/_8$ x $10\,^7/_8$ inches
176 pages, full color

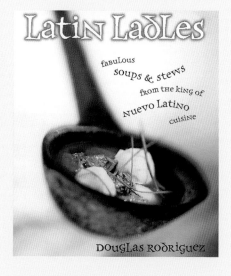

*Fabulous Soups & Stews from
the King of Nuevo Latino Cuisine*

$7\,^5/_{16}$ x $8\,^7/_8$ inches
144 pages, full color